The Charcoal Burner and Other Poems

兩鬢蒼蒼十指黑賣炭得錢何所營身
衣裳口中食可憐身上衣正單心憂炭
願天寒夜來城外一尺雪曉駕炭車輾
轍牛困人飢日已高市南門外泥中歇
翩翩兩騎來是誰黃衣使者白衫兒手把
書口稱勅迴車叱牛牽向北一車炭千
斤宮使驅將惜不得半疋紅綃一丈綾

The Charcoal Burner and Other Poems

Original Translations from the Poetry of the Chinese

Translated by Henry H. Hart

University of Oklahoma Press : Norman

The frontispiece is reproduced from "The Charcoal Burner" *in the original Chinese.*

By HENRY H. HART

A Chinese Market
The Hundred Names
The West Chamber
Seven Hundred Chinese Proverbs
A Garden of Peonies
Venetian Adventurer
Sea Road to the Indies
Poems of the Hundred Names
Luis de Camoëns and the Epic of the Lusiads
Marco Polo: Venetian Adventurer
The Charcoal Burner and Other Poems

Library of Congress Cataloging in Publication Data
Hart, Henry Hersch, 1886–1968   comp.
  The charcoal burner, and other poems.
  Bibliography: p.
  1. English poetry—Translations from Chinese. 2. Chinese poetry—Translations into English. I. Title.
PL2658.E3H28   895.1'1'008   73–19388
ISBN 0–8061–1185–2

Dedicated
to
Caroline Lilienthal Esberg
and
To the Memory
of
Sarah Lilienthal Wiel

PREFACE

Fortunately for China and for the Western world, with the passing of the years the volume of translations of Chinese poetry has been steadily increasing, and with the constant expansion of Chinese studies in European and American institutions of learning our understanding and appreciation of the Chinese mind and heart are becoming greater.

The Chinese poet, like the writer of lyrics in the West, reveals his spirit, his deepest emotions, his reactions and attitudes to life and to nature and toward his fellow man in his verse, whereas in prose he may remain objective, reticent, restrained or even impersonal and seemingly cold or austere.

The Confucian *Book of Poetry* (sometimes incorrectly called *The Book of Odes*), supposedly compiled and edited before Confucius, declares that "poetry may serve, among other things, to arouse emotion, help observation, and express one's grievances." The preface to the book, attributed to the Confucian scholar Pu Shang, avers that poetry has the power to make closer the tie between man and wife—and to deepen human relationships. More important to us, the same preface states that poetry follows the desires of the heart, expressing them in verse.

Despite several efforts in China and the Western world, no complete or adequate history of Chinese poetry as yet exists. However, one has no need of such a history to appreciate and enjoy Chinese lyrics in translation. The field has been sadly cluttered by paraphrases or by works of those pretending to know the language, who make so-called translations which are in no way translations either in the letter or the spirit, and by poems which have passed through several minds and hands after their presentation by the original translator.

The translations in this book, together with a brief introduction, seek to bring to the English-speaking reader various facets of China's life and poetic thought as expressed by some of her poets, from the fourth to the twentieth centuries A.D. Too many writers, Chinese as well as "foreign," have turned to the verse of the T'ang period, believing them to be the only poems worthy of study and translation. But the stream of Chinese poetry has ever been a rich, full, and unceasing one, reaching from very early antiquity to our own day, and the selections herein have been made from many centuries of Chinese life and experience.

The biographies of many Chinese poets, both men and women, have but scant interest for the average Western reader; therefore, biographical or anecdotal material has been held to a minimum, noted only when it may add interest to the poems themselves.

This volume will have served its purpose if it brings to the reader in English dress something of the life and culture, world outlook, charm, and beauty of that land which is still called by its people the "Middle Country," and above all if it gives, even though in translation (as near as the genius of the two languages will permit) a glimpse into the hearts and emotions, the dreams and hopes of the great Chinese people.

HENRY H. HART

CONTENTS

INTRODUCTION

The Content of Chinese Poetry

The Chinese cultural tradition in all its phases is far deeper and more widespread than that of the West. Even today, after over thirty-five centuries of war, conquest, and invasion, that tradition is largely an unbroken one of a people for the great part homogeneous. Their dwelling place has been China, where their experience has nurtured tradition which has become deeply rooted and their attitudes to life, nature, and art have grown, flourished, and become a part of them. The more we of the West learn of the underlying reactions to Chinese experience the more we can appreciate the Chinese poets and their work.

In their philosophy the Chinese have been realistic and pragmatic, and the successive events in their long history have brought them for the most part to an acceptance of what is, rather than a striving for that which, to our minds, should be. Thus the Chinese poets, we shall find, face life and its vicissitudes with far more resignation than do we of the Western world. They are in no way blind or indifferent to life's tragedy, the futility of war, the cruelty of man to man, the seeming hostility of nature. They see all these with eyes as clear as ours. The many and powerful protests against war fill pages of a Tu Fu; the emptiness and stupidity of pomp and power speak out in the lines of a Li Po and a Po Chü I; the sufferings of parting and exile, the pangs of vain or unrequited love find expression in the verses of a Wang Wei or Tzu Yeh. But the voices are muted, speaking of human tragedy in a low key—though nonetheless eloquent or moving in their restraint or understatement.

In the East as in the West human relations are all-important, but the actual experiences involved in them are not necessarily the same. Throughout the centuries the betrothal and marriage system of the Chinese has necessarily prevented love from manifesting itself on the part of either man or woman before marriage. Thus we seldom find in verse the pouring forth of the praises of the loved one, and great love poems are not the forte of the Chinese poet, though we find more of this material in the verses of the women poets. Such poems as express romantic love are in the main limited to those written to or for a husband or a wife or between those drawn to each other by ties other than marriage. Those that we do find, however, sing of passion as ardent as the love poems of the West, albeit more restrained and less bordering on the erotic, for in his poems, in contrast to his novels, the Chinese only hints at, rather than openly and frankly speaks of, his passion. We know that in his romances and stories he is often as explicit and carnal as his Western brother—and perhaps even more outspoken—but in his verse the poet seems to adhere to the wise adage that "it is of the nature of poetry not to say everything."[1]

Such love poems of the Chinese as we possess tell of the charms, the fidelity, and the enduring qualities and excellences of the loved one in such manner that beneath the surface is revealed the same love that dominates the relations of men and women found in the poetry of the West.

On the other hand, friendship between men appears in Chinese verse far more often and in more serious fashion than in the poetry of the West. The very nature of the relations between man and woman and of Chinese social, political, and economic experience easily explains this, as does the comparative failure of the Chinese to educate their women, save in exceptional cases, through the cen-

[1] Servius, *In Virgilii Aeneidos*, I, 683.

turies. In general, except for the *hetaerae*, education was exclusively the man's privilege. Consequently, his close associations throughout his formative years have largely been with those of his own sex, creating stronger ties of friendship and common experience than are usually found in our freer society. Educated Chinese very often sought employment in government service from very early times. Such a career necessitated separation from home and friends, for seldom was a man assigned to service in his home environment—a system designed primarily to prevent corruption or bribery, or, at the least, favoritism. The result was that an immense amount of Chinese poetry concerned itself with companionship between men, the sharing of intellectual and emotional experiences and reminiscences; regrets, heartaches, and grief at separation; longing for homecoming and reunion; and deprivation of the sharing of life. These sentiments inspired a vast number of China's finest lyrics.

The West has had its poets who have loved and written of Nature in all her moods, but it is doubtful that Western poetry has ever felt the immanence of Nature in all her manifestations down to the tiniest detail as have the Chinese. From the earliest times the Chinese have lived close to the soil, making them keen observers during all the days and ways of their lives. Little has escaped them, and from beginning to end their poems are saturated with Nature in her every season. This is so evident that it needs no further elaboration than the reading of any anthology of Chinese verse. There we find everywhere the mutations of the seasons, the benignity or the cruelty of natural phenomena. The poet seems to share his joys and sorrows, his hopes and fears, with a sentient Nature. This sympathy is all-embracing, from birds and insects to flowers, streams, rocks, and mountains. It so permeates Chinese poetry that it is often difficult to differentiate between man and his environment, so closely do they seem to share the scene.

In Chinese poetry we naturally find similes, allusions, and references to religion, philosophy, superstitions, legends, and folklore differing from those of the West. The mythology of southern Europe differs materially from that of the northern countries, but it is far more familiar to us than is that of China. Thus many Chinese literary references and devices may be unknown or obscure to the foreign reader, either in denotation or connotation or in both. For example, to the Chinese the moon implies loneliness, exile, and nostalgia. In Western mythology the Milky Way is the path of the gods; to the Chinese it is the celestial source of the Yellow River and recalls the tale of the Herdsman and his wife, the Spinning Lady. For us the sun is the chariot of Apollo, associated with the legends of Daedalus and Icarus. For the Chinese it is the abode of a three-legged red crow (or raven). One might continue indefinitely— stars have different tales for the Chinese, the flowers different attributes, the insects different symbolism.

Until we become accustomed to them, many similes, references, and comparisons, based on age-old customs and beliefs, seem recondite. Jade has no place in the Western poetical lexicon, yet it is ever ready at hand for the Chinese writer—a woman is as precious as jade, her hands and fingers are as delicate as jade, a talented young man is a tree of jade, the moon is a jade bracelet or a wheel of jade. The bamboo is ever present—the scholar is as smooth as bamboo, his life as regular as its spaced joints, his philosophy as pliant and flexible, bowing and bending, but not breaking when swept and tormented by the storms of life; the whole man is as universally useful as the bamboo stalk. The plum and the orchid are symbolic of a woman's virtue. The lotus speaks of the human soul; the green pine of eternity; the cicada of pure living and immortality and humility; the peach of life and health; each season a vivid symbol of human life and its changes, of decay and death.

The range of the symbolism of the Chinese in his life and poetry is broad beyond measure. But these divergences and traditional differences are of the mind, not of the heart. If and when we penetrate these differences, we realize that humanity is fundamentally the same everywhere and that in China, as in the West, deep calls to deep and understands. In all men the same emotions are stirred by the same causes—love, hate, sympathy, friendship, sorrow, and joy, and, once we allow for superficial differences, the brush of the Chinese poet brings to us the same messages as does the pen of the Western writer of verse.

The Stream of Chinese Poetry

The stream of Chinese culture, flowing full to overflowing through the centuries, has an unbroken tradition in comparison to the heritage of the West. This is everywhere evident in both the form and the content of its poetry. Until the irruption of the West into the East—and especially before the present world-upheavals—the internal and external outlook of the Chinese has varied but little through the centuries. That outlook, largely molded and deeply influenced through the ages by animism, Confucianism, Buddhism, and Taoism, has profoundly affected the direction, ideas, and forms of Chinese poetry.

If one begins his studies with the *Book of Songs*, traditionally over twenty-four hundred years old, and follows the various poets and their work down to the days of the Republic—and even beyond—he will find the stream broad, unbroken, and rich. The conquests, invasions, and internal convulsions that have filled Chinese history have not—at least until the present disturbed and fluid era—greatly affected the attitudes and modes of expression of her bards.[2] Suffice it here to note that women have contributed a goodly number of exquisite lyrics to the language. Little is known of most of these women—often we know no more than a name—but their contributions have been important ones, and no anthology would be complete without a generous number of these revelations of the mind and soul of Chinese women.

The Forms and Devices of Chinese Verse

Certain elements inherent in human speech are found in Chinese, as in all other poetry. The most important of these are rhyme, rhythm, and the varying length of lines and their arrangement within the poem. All these have been the objects of Chinese poetic experiment and usage. The tones of the language have, for poetic purposes, been reduced to two. Many intricate rhyme systems have been employed, though the monosyllabic nature of the language and its paucity of sounds precludes their reproduction in translation.[3]

A simplified classification of Chinese verse forms follows:

1. The *ku shih*, or ancient verses, which may be divided into
    a. Verse of four syllables
    b. Verses of five syllables
    c. Verses of seven syllables
    d. Verses of a variable number of syllables.

[2] For works on the history of Chinese poetry, see the Bibliography.
[3] Those interested in these techniques will find them fully discussed in Henry H. Hart (ed.), *Poems of the Hundred Names: A Short Introduction to Chinese Poetry*; and Arthur Waley, "Notes on Chinese Prosody," *Journal of the Royal Asiatic Society*, April, 1918.

2. The *lü shih*, or modern style, consisting of verses of five or seven syllables each.

In the five-syllable verses the caesura (pause) occurs after the second syllable of the verse; in the seven-syllable verse, after the fourth syllable. Poems are written in an even number of lines.

3. The *ch'ü*, dramatic verse, usually interspersed between prose lines in a play, roughly comparable to the aria in an opera, as contrasted to the *recitative*.

4. The *tzu*, a poem which traditionally was set to earlier or contemporary music. The lines of the *tzu* may vary in the number of syllables, and the number of lines in the poem may be irregular.[4]

Epic and tragic verse, as well as genuine narrative poetry, seldom occur in Chinese literature. There is, however, no lack of intensity of emotion, of profundity of thought, of quick and sensitive reaction of the heart and of spirit, all compressed into a few lines.

The structure of the Chinese language lends itself to this conciseness and intensity. Chinese is practically uninflected, its words being monosyllabic. It demands no indication of gender, number, tense, or case, and even the subject of the verb may often be omitted. In fact, Chinese is such a flexible, fluid language that a syllable may be a noun, a verb, an adjective, and so on, according to the exigencies of the occasion.

These considerations make it possible for the poet to reduce the expression of his thoughts, his impressions, and his emotions to the minimum and enable him to seize and

[4] When read aloud or recited, a Chinese poem is generally chanted, the caesura being slightly accented. The reading is staccato rather than legato, as in European reading, because of the nature of the language.

convey to us the very essence of his message, one that is timeless and universal.[5]

The famous lines of Blake may well be applied to the poets of China:

> To see a World in a Grain of Sand
> And Heaven in a Wild Flower,
> Hold Infinity in the palm of your hand
> And Eternity in an hour.

The Work of the Translator

Adding to the problems of the language, he who would translate correctly must have lived among the Chinese and acquired the faculty of seeing and thinking in Chinese, from the Chinese viewpoint. Moreover, he must, because of the subtlety of the characters, note their selection and use by the poet to convey his meaning—a selection which makes each poem a series of tiny vignettes, or minor poems within itself.

Perhaps a few illustrations will clarify this statement, and many more could be adduced. There are several characters which signify "morning," but the poet may desire to convey a more nearly exact picture to the reader's mind—and eye—by the character he uses for it. It must be remembered that Chinese characters were originally simple or complex word pictures, however they may have become altered in form, denotation, or connotation in the development of the language through the centuries. One character for "morning" may indicate "the sun is not yet visible"; another may convey the idea that "the sun is appearing over the mountain tops"; another that "there is an early mist

[5] It is this flexibility of the language that often produces more than one rendering of a line or an entire poem—and each can be a faithful translation.

with a fisherman in his boat"; another that "the rising sun strikes the helmet of the watchman as he leaves the wall after his night's vigil"; still another that "the sun appears above the tree tops"; another that "the time when the sun awakens and stirs animal life"; and yet another that "the rising sun casts its rays over the earth." These do not exhaust the denotations or connotations of the written character for this one idea. Thus the Chinese written language, rich in characters and character combinations, offers an infinite variety of color and nuance to the word painter whom we call the poet. Without pushing these interpretations too far, the translator should observe the choice of written characters and take them into account in his translation.

I hope that this introduction, brief as it is, will have opened the door sufficiently to afford at least a glimpse into the rich storehouse of Chinese poetry. Thousands of poems, long and short, both by the great masters and by obscure or unknown poets, still await the pen of the translator.[6] It would be pleasing also to think that this anthology, covering many facets of Chinese life and experience may, if only slightly, add to the pleasure and understanding of those who would grasp and comprehend the spirit of China as expressed in her poetry through the centuries.

[6] The imperial edition of the poems of the T'ang Dynasty (A.D. 618–922) alone contains over forty-eight thousand poems.

The Charcoal Burner
and Other Poems

GOLDEN VALLEY GARDEN

Anonymous

In the garden
Where once folk danced and sang,
None ever spoke of grass.
Today both dance and song
Have vanished,
And autumn's dew
Lies on the grass.

A PARTING GIFT

Lang Shih Yüan

In the early light of dawn,
When the gray-green clouds
And snow seemed to meet and merge,
From afar, borne on the north wind,
I hear the distressed cries
Of swallows and of geese.
Alas! Your friend is poor
And can offer you nought
As a parting gift
Save the far-off blue mountains
As I bid you farewell.

BRIEF REUNION

Li Yi

This is our first meeting since our youth,
After ten years of strife in the land.
I had to ask your name—though I recalled your face.
The evening bell found us still talking
Of the vast sea of events since last we parted.
Tomorrow you take the road to distant Pa Ling,
Beyond range upon range of autumn mountains.

WORDS

Liu Yü Hsi (772–842)

Li Yü Hsi was president of the Board of Rites.

> How oft do I bemoan the inability of words
> To express the deepest thoughts of man!
> Though you and I shall meet face to face
> At dawn,
> How, then, can we convey to each other
> The ten-thousand weighty reflections
> Of our hearts?

AUTUMN INSPIRATION

Liu Yü Hsi

From ancient times it has been said
That autumn days are desolate and sad,
But I believe that autumn days
Excel spring dawns.
See!
Just as the crane flies through the clouds
And soars on high,
So do I feel that the guiding spirit
Of my verse
Bears me to the blue heaven
On its wings.

THE BRIDGE OF CHU CH'IAO

Liu Yü Hsi

By the bridge of Chu Ch'iao
The grasses and flowers grow wild.
The evening sun casts long shadows
Upon the road.
Where once stood the stately halls of kings
The swallows now flit to and fro
Among the homes of humble folk.

THE WINDS OF AUTUMN

Liu Yü Hsi

Whence comes this wind of autumn?
Its whistling blast
Drives the flocks of wild geese
In headlong flight.
At dawn it invades the courtyard
To assail the trees
—But the solitary wanderer
Hears its mournful howling first of all.

JEALOUS

Meng Hao

You wish to go,
But I cling to your robe.
To what place are you going?
I am not disturbed
That you may return late
—But whom are you going to meet?

THE PLUM BLOSSOM

T'ao Shih

The sounds of the sheng and the drum
Have died away,
Leaving my spirit distressed and sad.
Then, as I sit in the upper room
And watch the moon
Ascend the heavens,
Of a sudden a gentle breeze
Stirs a branch of the plum,
... And a blossom opens
For me alone.

LOVE

Wu Yung

One yearns for the other.
How two draw together!
It is tenuous
As a silken thread
And as deep as the sea.
Ah! The moon is not always round,
And flowers soon fade.
Life has brought me many heartaches
—And ah, how many for her!

NIGHT RAIN

Yin Shih (a woman poet)

The autumn wind
Sighs through the yellow grass;
The fine rain
Drips from the pines;
The flame in the solitary lamp
Sputters and dies;
The fallen leaves rustle
In heaps,
... And a bird calls
At my window.

THE UNANSWERABLE RIDDLE

Han Shan (a monk)

The height of heaven is infinite;
The volume of earth beyond all measure.
In these elements exist all living creatures.
A creative force has brought them forth
And ever influences them by its strength.
They struggle to obtain their ends
For the very food they eat.
Of all this conflict who can judge
Its cause and its effect?
A blind child may as well ask,
"What is the color of milk?"

THE SPAN OF LIFE

Han Shan

A man's life does not fill a hundred years,
But his cares may be enough for a thousand.
First come his own illnesses,
Then the woes of his family—sons and grandsons.
He examines the roots of his grains
And the topmost boughs of his mulberry trees.
An iron hammer,
If it falls into the eastern sea,
Finds no rest
Until it reaches the bottom.

THE SPIRIT OF MAN

Han Shan

Oh, seeker after the Way,
You who are weary with striving,
I declare unto you
That in man dwells a spirit
Not definable in words
Nor acquired by learning.
Though hidden, it will appear
And answer when summoned.
I enjoin you, be zealous,
Watch and guard it well.
Let there never be a stain to defile it.

THE FOUR SEASONS

T'ao Ch'ien (365–427)

Spring enriches all four corners of the land
With its waters.
Summer clouds clothe the mountains
In rarest beauty.
Autumn's moon floods the whole scene
With its glory.
Winter brings forth lone pines
Upon the hills.

THE PHILOSOPHER

T'ao Ch'ien

I have built my hut
In the midst of men,
But no clamor, no noise of horse or cart
Disturbs me.
You ask how this can be?
It is because my heart is far removed,
And I keep myself apart.
From the eastern hedge I pick chrysanthemums
And look up at the southern mountains.
On the hills the air is fresh both day and night.
The birds and I keep pace together.
It is among these realities
That truth does dwell.
Would that I could explain this,
But the words to do so
Quite escape me.

THE FAN

Tzu Yeh

Tzu Yeh was a woman poet of the Ch'in Dynasty. Of her poems 150 have survived, but little is known of her life.

> You hold in your hand
> A round white fan,
> Pure as the autumn moon.
> You have but to wave it,
> And it conveys
> The message of your affection
> Without words.

DISTRAUGHT

Tzu Yeh

Ever since I returned
From bidding you farewell,
I have been weeping.
My dressing case stands unopened;
I have not the courage to touch it.
My hair remains disheveled,
For I have no inclination
To arrange it,
Nor to brush off the dust
That gathers on my yellow robe.

GRIEF

Tzu Yeh

In the morning
As I go out before the door,
I am sad,
And in the evening
When I return,
My grief is with me still.
I talk and laugh with the passers-by,
But within me
My heart is inconsolable,
Recalling you.

LONGING

Tzu Yeh

Since you have gone,
The glittering frost of day
Has become
As the darkness of the night.
I cannot keep my thoughts
From you,
When the wind sweeps down,
Or when the shadows come and go.

A HAUNTING MELODY

Tzu Yeh

The strings and bamboo instruments
Burst into song,
And the air is filled with clearest sound.
The tune is all unknown to me.
It is full of mystery,
But its power and its virtue pass direct
From the singer
Into the heart of him who listens.

PEACH BLOSSOMS

Tzu Yeh

When in spring
The peach bursts forth incarnadine
Ah! how we cherish it,
Love its color,
Guard its blossom carefully.
But when the flowers of summer
Fall and vanish,
Who gives them a thought,
Who seeks for them again?

SHADOWS

Tzu Yeh

Since your departure
The night is bright with brilliant frost.
My thoughts of you are like shadows in the wind.
They come, they go,
But are unceasing, ever recurring,
And I can do nought
To stop them.

SPRING LONGING

Tzu Yeh

When on the steps
Incense stirs the emotions
And in the courtyard
Flowers delight the eye
—When these arouse spring's desires,
Human nature cannot be denied.

THE EMPTY ROOM

Tzu Yeh

Since you have gone,
The room
With its light gauze curtains
Stands empty.
My thoughts of you
Are as a portrait,
Lighted bright with candles—
But longing for you
Makes my eyes grow dim.

VOICES IN THE NIGHT

Tzu Yeh

The night is long,
And I seek sleep in vain.
How bright the moon gleams!
I imagine
I hear voices calling,
But the sounds are unreal,
Hollow
—And no answer comes.

HEARTACHE

Chang Chiu Ling (673–740)

Chang Chiu Ling was a statesman under Hsüan Tsung
(Ming Huang), of the T'ang Dynasty. He was one of the
brilliant poets of the era.

> Since you have left me,
> Reason cannot change
> My sense of loss.
> I am as the moon
> On the night of its full,
> Whose light and glory
> Thenceforth diminish
> And grow dimmer
> With each day.

DREAMS

Chang Chiu Ling

The bright moon rises out of the sea.
In the heaven's vast expanse
The hour is everywhere the same.
Nightfall is the saddest time of day,
For then my heart yearns for my beloved,
As I know she longs for me.
Waiting for the coming of the dawn,
I put out my candle,
Then dream of blissful meeting with her,
So far away.

ALONE

Chin Feng Chi

Since you have left my side,
Grief and melancholy
Have driven all color
From my cheek.
—But then,
When my thoughts turn to you,
It is as though a bright candle
Were lighted in my heart
—And I control my tears.

A PICTURE

Kung Weng Kuai (Liang Dynasty)

A beautiful maid
Sits by her window
The livelong spring day.
She preens herself
Before her shining mirror,
Carefully arranging her arched moth eyebrows
—Herself like a blossom newly opened,
Her hands delicate as jade.
A swallow swoops down
To seize on a seed
From the shallow pool in the garden.
A breeze gently stirs
In the willows.
The maid's thoughts are of you:
"When will you return,
That we may share a cup of wine together?"

RETURN

Ho Chih Chang

Ho Chih Chang was a minister of Ming Huang, of the T'ang Dynasty. He was one of the "Eight Immortals of the Wine Cup." This poem was written about 659.

I was but a youth
When I left my village,
And now I return,
Full of years.
My accent is no longer the same,
And my hair is gray and thin.
When they meet me,
My children know me not
And mock me, asking,
"Stranger, from what place do you come?"

THE GENERATIONS OF MAN

Ch'en Tzu Ang (656–98)

Ch'en Tzu Ang was a statesman under Empress Wu Hou of the T'ang Dynasty. He died in prison.

Looking back,
I cannot see the men of old
Or, looking forward,
Those of the years to come.
When I reflect and meditate
On the unending years
Of sky and earth,
I stand in solitude
And shed despairing tears.

NIGHTFALL

Ch'en Tzu Ang

Slowly, slowly
Bright day fades into dusk;
In sighs
The autumn wind rises.
The glory of our years
Declines and sinks,
And what is the end
Of all our hopes and dreams?

ON CHI HILL

Ch'en Tzu Ang

Traveling southward
I rode up to Chieh Chih,
And from afar I saw the Golden Tower.
The mounds about were overgrown with trees,
But vanished were all traces
Of the palace and the monarch.
I reflected on his schemes and plans
—How futile they were,
And all gone awry.
Then, putting spurs to my horse,
I galloped on my way.

TWILIGHT ON OMEI[1]

Li Po (Li T'ai-po, *ca.* 700–62)

Li Po, who lived during the T'ang Dynasty, was probably
China's greatest poet. He was one of the band called the
"Eight Immortals of the Wine Cup."

From Omei's southern slope
Descends a monk with his green-stringed lute.
He plays for me,
And the sound is as the wind
In ten thousand pines
In the valley below.
It purifies the wanderer's heart
As though it were plunged
In the clearest stream.
Its dying echoes arouse a frosty note
In a nearby temple bell.
The sun sinks down behind the hills,
Their peaks blotted out
By autumn's dark-green clouds
—But of this I am unaware.

[1] Omei is one of the Chinese peaks sacred to Buddhist pilgrims.
It rises steeply ten thousand feet from the plain of Szechwan. There
are fifty-six pagodas and over seventy temples and monasteries on the
mountain, with over two thousand monks—or were before the Com-
munist era.

ANXIETY

Li Po

The moon is waning
Over Changan,[1]
And in ten thousand homes
I heard the thud
Of the washing paddles.
—And all the time
The winds of autumn never cease.
My heart is at the far frontier.
On what day
Will the dread barbarians of the north be destroyed?

[1] Sian, a city in Shensi Province.

THE BIVOUAC

Li Po

'Tis the fifth month,
But the snow still lingers
On Tai Shan.[1]
There no flowers ever grow in the cold,
And even were one to play "The Spring Willow"
On his flute,
Spring would make no display
Of its colors.
In the dark of night
We sleep with arms in hand
And saddles ready at our sides.
At dawn the war drums summon us
To battle.
Would that I could unsheathe my sword
And slay Lou Lan,
Who draws us on
To death!

[1] A sacred mountain in Shantung Province.

A DRINKING BOUT

Li Po

We have been drinking among the flowers
—First one cup, then another,
Cup following cup,
Until I am quite overcome with wine
And fain would sleep.
It is better that you go.
But, if you wish,
Come back tomorrow
—And bring your lute with you.

THE FIREFLY

Li Po

Rainstorms could do little
To dim your light,
And the winds
But make your lantern
All the brighter glow.
If you should wing your flight
Up near the moon,
I am sure you would twinkle
As a star.

A FRUITLESS VISIT TO A TAOIST PRIEST

Li Po

Amid the sounds of running water
A dog barks.
There has been a heavy rain
On the peach blossoms hereabouts.
From time to time I glimpse a deer
In the deep woods.
The green of the wild bamboo contrasts
With the bright white clouds.
The waterfalls hang
As though draped on the green peaks.
No one knows whither the priest has gone.
Regretfully I recline among the scattered pines.

THE IMPERIAL GUARD

Li Po

Twelve leaders of the Imperial Guard march by.
Their robes of gauze outshine the stars
In splendor.
Beneath the harvest moon their weapons glitter
As the frost,
And the varicolored banners are
As the rainbows
Against the evening clouds.
While the troops file by,
Ten thousand doors are closed
In respect to majesty.
The solemn martial music soars
To the ninth heaven,
And the breeze plays gently about the person
Of our sovereign lord.

IN MY CUPS

Li Po

Bemused by wine,
I noticed not the creeping on of night.
The flowers had showered their petals
On my robe.
I rose, staggered, and walked along the bank
Of the moonlit stream.
The birds had gone to rest,
And of men but few were stirring.

THE INN AT GIN LING

Li Po

The breeze fills the inn
With the scent of willow blossoms.
The young people of Gin Ling have come
To greet and bid their friends farewell.
A handsome Soochow girl
Repeatedly fills their cups
And urges them to drink.
Toasts are proposed
Both to those remaining and to those departing.
You, sir,
I pray you ask of the river flowing east
If he knows of any parting
As long or as constant
As his.

INVASION

Li Po

In Yen Chih
When the yellow leaves fall,
I look afar from my terrace
To where you may be.
The gray clouds from the sea
Are stilled;
The gloomy hue of autumn
Descends on my spirit.
In the desert waste of Gobi[1]
The Tartar hordes block the frontier;
The soldiers of Han[2] retreat
To the Ten Thousand Li Wall,[3]
And in the day of battle
Many a loved one is lost.
My heart is empty and sad;
I am but an orchid,
Broken on its stem.

[1] Gobi means "desert."
[2] China.
[3] The Chinese name for the Great Wall.

THE JADE FLUTE

Li Po

Whence,
From what concealed jade flute
Come those dulcet notes,
Borne on the soft breeze of spring?
The music, now rising, now falling,
In muted accents,
Seems to fill the streets of Lo Yang.
Who is it?
In what secret old garden
Is he thus pouring out his heart,
To what lovely willow-waisted maiden?

LODGING ON THE MOUNTAIN

Li Po

The twilight creeps down
Over the green mountain,
And the moon follows our homeward-bound footsteps.
We gaze at the road by which we have come
As it winds back over the hills.
Walking hand in hand,
We reach the rude cottage,
Where a young boy
Opens the thornwood gate for us.
The bamboo, bending over,
Makes the pathway gloomy,
And the green vines catch at our clothes.
Gladly we say, "Here we can rest."
The goodly wine drives our care away.
We sing in praise of the pine-laden breeze,
And drink
Until the river of stars grows dim in the sky.
We are intoxicated with the sheer joy of living,
And forget all the woes of the world.

NAN HU

Li Po

The autumn sun
Shines bright
On the green waters
Of Nan Hu.
A man in a boat
Gathers white duckweed.
All the while
Sweet lotus
Gives forth its tantalizing perfume,
Stirring him strangely
Until he is sad unto death.

A SOLDIER TO HIS WIFE

Li Po

'Tis autumn,
The time when raiders ride down from the north
To ravage the land.
From the dwellings of Han
Men are summoned to arms.
Messengers are dispatched;
The army bivouacs on the sand.
The very shadow of the moon
Is the shape of a bow.
Our men polish the flowers
Of Tartar frost
From their swords.
We have not yet fought our way
Through the Great Wall.
Ah, little wife,
Heave not such long sighs!

A THOUGHT OF SPRING

[From a Wife to a Husband]

Li Po

The grass of Yen
Is like jade-green silk;
The mulberry trees in Ch'in
Bow their verdant branches low.
At this time, my love,
Your heart
Surely turns toward home.
And mine?
It is about to break.
Breezes of spring,
I recognize you not.
Why do you enter
My curtains of gauze?

THE TRAVELERS

Li Po

We have come as strangers
From far Hupeh
And crossed the river
Beyond Ching Man.
The mountains have dwindled into plains,
And the rivers draw near to the sea.
The moon shines down
From the mirror of heaven,
And the clouds build up castles
In the sea.
How we love the streams
Of our faraway land,
Whence boats have brought us
Ten thousand li!

TUNG SHAN

Li Po

'Tis many a day
Since last I climbed Tung Shan's peak.
How often since then
Have the red roses bloomed on its slope!
Unobserved of man,
Its clouds scatter.
On whose home
Do the bright moonbeams fall?

THE WIFE

Li Po

Near the town of Huang Yün
The crows come to roost;
They light on the branches
And call, "Ya, Ya."
At her loom
Sits a woman of Ch'in Ch'ien,
Weaving a silk brocade.
Her window is draped
In jade-green gauze, light as smoke.
She speaks,
Then, overwhelmed
By the thoughts of her faraway husband,
She arrests her shuttle,
And,
Because she must sleep alone each night
In an empty room,
Her tears fall,
Heavy as rain.

HOMESICK

Tu Fu (712–70)

Tu Fu, who lived during the T'ang Dynasty, was one of China's greatest poets. He was the subject of a number of biographies and studies in many languages. He was an ardent antimilitarist, expressing his views in many of his verses. Though he served in public office, he preferred a wandering life.

In the willows
Two yellow orioles are singing,
And across the azure sky
Wings a flight of wild egrets.
Sadly I look from my window
Toward the southern mountain range,
Where lie the suns
Of a thousand autumns.
In my thoughts
I pass out through my door
To the land of Wu,
My home with its ships,
Ten thousand li away.

AN OLD MAN'S WANDERING THOUGHTS

Tu Fu

This afternoon the village was startled
By a sudden wind.
The rain in passing
Drenched the gloomy courtyard,
But the grass has steamed dry
In the sunshine of evening.
The light from the distant river
Is reflected through my curtain.
My books now lie in disarray.
Who can arrange them?
My cup is dry.
I can fill it myself.
I often hear too much conversation.
I wonder if I, an old man,
Had better talk less!

DAWN IN THE MOUNTAINS

Tu Fu

In Po Tu
No longer is heard the tap
Of the night watch;
On Yang T'ai Hill
Slowly the darkness pales into dawn.
On the high peaks
The chill sun begins to glow,
Though beyond the mountain range
The damp clouds still slumber on.
Up over the earth's brim
Silently glides a tiny sail.
All is so still
That even the fall of a leaflet
Is heard.
Before my thorn-woven gate
Pass two deer.
Ah, I should like
To mingle with your herd.

THE ESCAPED PRISONER

Tu Fu

There are red clouds in the west
Over the lofty peaks
As the sun sets toward the plains.
The swallows twitter at the brushwood gate.
I am home at last,
After a journey of a thousand li.
My wife and little ones are startled
To see me,
And, even when reassured,
They wipe away a furtive tear.
What time the world was swept by anarchy
I was carried off a prisoner—
But life, by merest chance
Brings me to my home again.
The wall is lined with our neighbors' heads,
All moved to sighs and sobs of thankfulness.
Until far into the night
We gather round the candle's flame
As though asleep, or in a dream.

FAREWELL

Tu Fu

Heaven and earth are crowded
With men in battle dress.
Family and friends all wept as one
When you saddled your horse
And rode off to the city
Beleagured by the Mongol horde.
The trees and the grass will change,
The long months and years will come and go,
And on the northern frontier
The freezing snow will lie
On the rivers.
Though it was but yesterday
That you left us,
We can already realize
That thus were touched also
The hearts of the men of old.

FROM EXILE

Tu Fu

Over the blue stream
The white birds
Wing their flight,
And the flowers
Blaze red
On the green hillside.
Now I know
That another spring has passed.
Ah! On what day
Will my years of exile end?

THE GOODLY RAIN

Tu Fu

The goodly rain
Knows its time and seasons.
Born in the spring,
It moves with the wind;
Clothing itself in the night,
It enriches all things.
In silence, but in fullest measure,
Its clouds
Hide the mountain paths
With their darkness;
The lantern on the boat in the river
Alone shines forth bright.
Dawn finds all drenched in the city,
And the flowers are a tapestry
Fit for a temple
Or palace.

A GUEST ARRIVES

Tu Fu

It is spring.
The stream flows north and south
Before my hut.
Only flocks of gulls call each day
To see me.
I have not swept the fruit blossoms
From the path for any visitor,
And my wicker gate opens today
For the first time for you.
The market is far away,
So I have no great variety of food
To offer you.
My home is poor,
So my jar of wine is of an old brew.
If you wish my neighbor to sit with us,
I shall call to him over the fence
And invite him
To share the cupfuls that remain.

THE LEADER TO HIS MEN

Tu Fu

Draw your bows,
Bend them with force.
Choose your arrows with care,
Be sure they are long.
Pick your man,
But shoot his horse first.
Seize your opponents
But first take their king.
Cease the slaughter
Once the country is yours.
Stop all aggression,
Prevent all invasion
—But remember,
In too much killing
Is irreparable wrong.

A LETTER TO JUDGE YANG

Tu Fu

All were asleep on the houseboat
Moored at the sandy bank
And gracefully aswing with the current.
Suddenly a storm arose.
The lamp was blown out.
Confusion ensued.
As the rain unceasing fell,
The river became a roaring torrent.
When we were aroused by the temple bell
In the early dawn,
The banks were streaming.
Dark clouds obscured the sun,
And gray mist veiled far Shih Tang.
Silently we rowed away from the seagulls' haunts.
Thus I could not reach you.
Deeply disappointed am I,
Knowing, sir, your wisdom and your worth.

LODGING FOR THE NIGHT

Tu Fu

The yu t'ung trees by the wall
In the army office courtyard
Seem chilled.
I am lodged alone in the river town,
And my candle is burning low.
Through the night that seems eternal
The signal horns speak out
One to another in mournful tones.
Who is there
To look out upon the lovely colored moon
In mid-heaven?
The long-drawn-out upheaval
Has cut off all communication,
And travel through the barren frontier passes
Is most toilsome.
After enduring ten years of work and worry
I have, though half-unwillingly,
Come here
To perch upon this single peaceful branch.

MOONLIGHT

Tu Fu

Tonight my wife is alone,
Watching the moon shine down on Fu Chou.
My heart aches for my little children far away.
They cannot understand
About their father in Changan.
My wife's cloudlike hair
Must be damp with the fragrant mist,
And her jadelike arms chilled
By the cold moonlight.
When shall we once more lean together
At the open window to look upon the moon,
While the traces of tears of happiness
Dry on our cheeks?

NIGHT THOUGHTS

Tu Fu

Tufts of grass on the bank
Stirred by the breeze.
A lone boat,
A tall mast in the night.
Stars hanging low
Over wild land and tilled field.
Moonlight shimmering
On the swift-flowing Great River.
How can I win fame
By the work of my pen?
Worn out in public service,
I am wiser to resign.
Tossed about
In the whirlwinds of life,
What am I?
A seagull, hovering
'Twixt heaven and earth!

ON HEARING THAT THE IMPERIAL ARMY
HAS RECOVERED HONAN AND HOPEH

Tu Fu

The report comes to us outside Chien
Of the retaking of Chi Pei.
When first I heard it, I wept with joy
Until my robe was wet with tears.
I turn and look at my wife and children,
—And where can sorrow be?
Carelessly I roll up my book of verse
And am frantic in my ecstasy.
Though it is broad daylight,
I must sing and drink.
I want to return to my far-off home
With green spring as my comrade.
I shall travel by the gorge of Pa
To the gorge of Wu
And thence by way of Hsiang Yang
To Lo Yang.

PASTORAL

Tu Fu

The metal curtain fittings gleam
In the setting sun.
Spring daylight fades to gloom.
The perfume of the orchard
Is wafted from the bank.
The wood gatherers have moored their boat
And cook their meal
Upon the sand.
The birds
That scream and fight for place
On the bough
Totter and fall.
In the garden
Floats a cloud of insects
In the air.
Oh, turbid lees of wine,
Who thus created you,
So that a single cup
Can dispel a thousand griefs?

REVERIE

Tu Fu

The moss-grown path leads through the bamboo grove
Down to the stream.
The flowers, shaded by the chestnut-wood eaves,
Have opened in the warm spring sun.
Full sixty years have flown
Since I last was here.
I lean upon my staff
And gaze once more at the solitary peak,
Then empty the dregs of my wine pot
On the sand.
Far out on the peaceful waves
The seagulls float
And the swallows fly slanting
Into the adverse wind.
Each generation of men has trod its own thorny path,
And my life, too, has had its disillusions.
So this old body wakes,
Then drinks its fill again
—And wherever I chance to find myself,
There I make my home.

SHIH HAO

[An Incident of the Civil War]
Tu Fu

The twilight was creeping
Over the hamlet of Shih Hao.
I heard the soldiers come
To seize the old man.
He—a grandfather—climbed over the wall
And fled.
His wife went to the door
To meet them.
They shouted at her in anger,
And she answered them in bitterness.
She had, she said, three sons,
All forced to take up arms.
They had fought at Yeh Town.
The youngest had written
That two were dead
And that he had hardly escaped alive.
Then she cried aloud,
"Alas, the dead are long dead, dead forever!
Inside the house
Are only my grandson, a babe at the breast,
And his mother,
In such rags that she cannot be seen."
The soldiers ordered that she go with them
Through the night and that she make haste.
As she quickly cooked some food,
I heard her weep, smothering her sobs.

When the sun rose bright the following morn,
I continued on my way.
There I met the old man
And bade him farewell.

A SOLDIER'S LETTER

Tu Fu

On the frontier
The war drums roll;
The men are on the march.
It is autumn,
And henceforth
The nightly dew will be white,
Though in my homeland
The moon shines bright.
All my brothers are scattered far,
With none at home
To ask if they yet live.
Letters I write.
Long I wait,
But no answers come.
Ah, how uncertain
Is the life of a soldier!

THUS PASSETH THE GLORY OF THIS WORLD

Tu Fu

At the bend in the river
The pine tree bends before the blast.
A mouse skulks among the ancient broken tiles
Of the long-forgotten palace.
The will-o'-the-wisp lurks in the dim, dank corners
Of the halls.
In the roar of wind and rain
I seem to hear the notes
Of sheng and bamboo flute.
Proud women who once adorned these storied rooms
Are now but yellow earth,
Their perfume boxes but broken shards
Beneath my feet,
And where once the great prince
Drove his gilded chariot
Now stands his tomb,
A moss-grown horse of stone thereon.
He who would sing the dirge of the long-dead prince
Must stand upon the withered grass
And mingle the sad music with his welling tears
And know once more that oblivion is the lot
Of all mankind,
For, no matter how great their fame,
They vanish with the steady marching
Of the years.

TAI SHAN

Tu Fu

What shall I say of Tai Shan?[1]
Here the states of Ch'i and Lu
Survive and flourish.
Here all unite to create and nourish
A grace and spirit.
Here Yang and Yin appear at dusk and dawn.
Looking to the heights
That soar far above the clouds
Makes one's breast swell in wonderment.
From it one sees the flight of birds
That come and go,
And when one ascends the topmost peak of all,
The other mountains in the land
Seem small indeed.

[1] Tai Shan, in Shantung Province, is the principal sacred peak of China. The summit is reached by a stone stairway of nearly seven thousand steps, bordered by temples, monuments, and shrines. The chief deity was a goddess, Pi Hsia Yüan Chün, Goddess of the Dawn. At the top are the temple to Yü Huang, the "Jade Emperor," the supreme god of Taoism, and a Confucian temple.

TAKE ADVANTAGE OF TODAY

Tu Fu

A single petal fluttering from the branch
Detracts but little from the beauty of the spring.
But when full ten thousand are torn away,
It saddens the heart of man,
For then he knows
That spring is doomed to die.
But time recks not of man's distress and woe
Or if it destroys for the nonce
His eager thirst for wine.
Let the kingfisher nest in his garden,
And the stone unicorn stand high on his hill.
If we are wise
And let reason guide,
We shall forget the frail bubble of fame,
Cast aside man's ambitions,
And seize happiness here and today.

WAR

Tu Fu

Though a country is ravished,
The mountains and rivers remain.
Though the grass and the trees are dense,
At such times the very flowers
Seem to weep.
And with hearts full of woe
The birds take to flight.
For three long months without ceasing
The beacon fires burn.
Letters from home
Cost countless coins to send.
My white hair grows thin with care,
And my pen cannot master
My thoughts so confused.

YO YANG TOWER

Tu Fu

Long ago I heard of Tungting Lake,
And today I have climbed Yo Yang Tower.
The lake cuts the lands of Wu and Ch'u
To east and south.
The sky and earth float day and night
In its waters.
From family and friends I have had no word.
A sick old man, I possess but a single boat.
The soldiers ride north of the passes.
I lean on the balcony
And weep.

POUNDING THE CLOTHES

Tu Fu

I know it will be long
Ere you return from war.
Autumn is at hand,
And I must scrub the washing stone anew.
Soon the bitter months of chill winter
Will be here,
And this time of separation
Weighs each day more heavily on my heart.
To pound these clothes is weary toil indeed,
But I must haste to send them to you
At the Great Wall so far away.
It exacts all my woman's strength
—And I wonder
If you can hear the pounding echo
Where you are!

SENTRIES

Li-i (eighth century)

Li-i was president of the Board of Rites. Many of his poems
were set to music.

On Hui Lo Peak
The sand lies white as snow;
The moonlight is as frost.
Before the walls
Of Shou Chiang Town
Comes the distant note
Of a Tartar pipe.
—But our sentries long
For their homes afar.

TOO LATE!

Li-i

I am married to a Ch'ü T'ang trader.
Every day that passes I realize my mistake.
If only I had known earlier
That I could trust in the tides,
I would have chosen a lad from the river!

THE WATER CLOCK

Li-i

The fragrance of the spring blossoms
Is but increased
By the gathering dew.
From the Chao Yang palace
Comes the sound of song
In the bright moonlight.
For me
The water clock drips so slowly
That it seems to contain the sea,
And its maddening "patter, patter"
Never ceases
Through the night.

THE WORLD AND I

Wang Wei (699–759)

Wang Wei was a poet, physician, painter, and statesman. Widowed at thirty-one, he never remarried. He was the founder of the Southern Sung school of painting.

When I was in my middle years
I devoted myself to Taoist lore,
But now, in later life,
I have returned to my home
On the Nan Shan frontier.
When the mood seizes me
I wander here alone
To escape the affairs of the world
And become acquainted with myself.
I follow the streamlet to its source;
I watch the clouds drift in the sky,
And perhaps, when in the woods I meet a friend,
We talk and laugh
And give no heed
To the passing of the hours.

AUTUMN

Wang Wei

After the new rains have deluged the mountains,
The weather changes in autumn.
The moon shines bright
Among the pines,
And the clear stream splashes loudly
On its stones.
In the bamboos
Echoes the chatter of the washerwomen
Returning home;
The boat of the fisherman
Disturbs the lotuses.
Though the fragrance of spring
Has passed away,
There remains much
To delight the eye
—Even of a prince.

THE YANGTZE GORGES

Wang Wei

It is late spring.
At early dawn we reach the gorge of Pa,
And my thoughts hark back
To the capital city of Changan.
A woman washes by the shining riverbank,
And in the morning sun
A multitude of birds is singing.
This is a land of waters,
Where peasants carry on their traffic
In their boats.
Some gorges are so deep
That from the bridges we can see but treetops.
At times we climb so high
That we glimpse ten thousand waterfalls.
The people speak in a tongue unknown to us
—But, ah, the oriole's song remains the same,
And here is so much of beauty in mountain
And in water
That it lessens the tug of our heartstrings
For our home.

MY MOUNTAIN HOME

Wang Wei

Opposite Chung Nan Mountain
Stands my thatched cottage.
For a whole year
No guest has lifted my latch.
I pass entire days alone
At leisure;
There is no one to interrupt
My drinking of wine
Or casting my hook for fish.
But come!
You are ever welcome,
To come and to come again.

A LONG JOURNEY

Wang Wei

The air on the palace moat
Is thin and chill.
I draw rein
And look out upon the mountains
In their majesty and beauty.
Alas, that I must ride so far alone!

AUTUMN

Wang Wei

The barren mountains are becoming blue-green,
And each day the autumn floods increase.
Leaning on my staff, I stand outside my door
And listen to the cicadas shrill
In the evening breeze.
The sun is setting down by the ford.
The smoke rises from the scattered village roofs.
I feel revived with drink
And wildly sing "Under the Five Willow Trees."

THE HUNT

Wang Wei

The general and his men ride forth
Through the town of Wei.
The strings of their horn bows
Hum in the strong wind.
See the horses gallop fast
Across the plain,
Where the snow has vanished,
The keen eye of the hawk
Watching from on high!
An eagle is killed.
They return to the camp
In the sunset,
The sky overcast
With black clouds.

THE EVENING OF OUR YEARS

Wang Wei

The evening of our years
Seeks peace and quiet,
Unaffected
By the outside world of men
—And we should have no plans
For distant futures.
In our leisure
Let us then revisit
The forests of our youth.
Let us loosen our girdles
To the pine-laden breeze
And invite the moon above the hilltops
To shine on us
As we pluck the strings of our lutes.
Surely you do not seek
To master all man's knowledge.
Hark!
The fishermen are singing
On the riverbank.

A VISIT

Wang Wei

You dismounted
And drank wine with me.
I inquired
Whither you were riding.
You answered
That your plans had failed
And that you were returning
To the southern mountain frontier.
I questioned no more, and you departed.
The white clouds have never found repose
In time or space.

THE GARDEN

Wang Wei

You find it strange
That the door of my boudoir
Is ever closed
And that in the court we meet no more?
It is because I am always
In the "Garden of the Spring,"
There learning the language
Of the smiling flowers.

A VISION

Po Chü-i (772–846)

Po Chü-i was one of China's greatest poets. A member of
the Han Lin Academy, he rose to high rank, but was sud-
denly and inexplicably exiled to Chiang Chou as magis-
trate. Later he was recalled and appointed governor of
Hangchow and then of Soochow. He ended his public ser-
vice as president of the Board of War. By imperial com-
mand his poems were engraved on stone tablets and set up
in a garden designed by the poet himself.

A flower
—Yet not a flower,
A mist
—Yet not a mist.
At midnight you came forth
And vanished with the dawn.
You appeared as a dream
In the springtime,
Transient as a cloud,
Dissolving without trace
In the morning sun.

THE SCHOLAR

Po Chü-i

Pity then the scholar, the diligent student.
He ignores fatigue; he reads his books
Until his eyes lose their luster.
He uses his brush until his fingers are calloused.
Ten times or more he is examined
Before he attains fame.
Bitterness indeed!
Even if at last he reaches success,
His hair is already thin as silk.
Pity for the days of his vigorous youth,
For they are exhausted in study.
When at last he has climbed to the summit
And has become a man of renown,
He can hold it but lightly.

THE HAIRPIN

Po Chü-i

In the lake
The water chestnuts intertwine with the lotus
And nod and flutter in the wind.
In a small boat
Deep in the midst of the blossoms
Her lover comes to meet her.
She desires to speak to him
And laughingly tosses her head.
See!
Her green jade hairpin has fallen
Into the deep water of the pool!

WAR'S CONSEQUENCES

Po Chü-i

Times are hard;
Trade is dead.
The whole year has been barren and waste.
Brothers, once united, are separated;
Some have gone east, others west.
Gardens and fields are deserted and bleak
Where a thousand spears have passed.
On the roadside
Are scattered the people's flesh and bones.
Their specters wail high above the earth
As wild geese in their flight,
And, disembodied,
They hover in tangled shapes
Through the autumn night.
But when they see the bright moon rise,
Their tears pour down like rain,
And all through the dark hours
In their sad, sad hearts
They long to be in their homes once more!

OLD VERSES

Po Chü-i

'Tis late in the night.
I cease reading
And close my book of verse
With a long, long sigh.
As I sit before my lamp,
The tears fall fast upon my old white beard.
I wrote those poems full twenty years ago,
But of the companions
Who drank and sang with me
Nine of every ten
Will never foregather
With me again.

NIGHT SNOW

Po Chü-i

Startled,
I find my pillow and my coverlet
Suddenly grow chill.
Deep in the night
My window seems bright.
I hear the bamboo stems break noisily
Under the weight of the snow.

DESERTED

Po Chü-i

Fragrance rising
From the jade incense bowl,
Red candles slowly dropping their waxen tears,
I, tossing all night on my pillow chill,
My hair grown gray and my eyebrows thin;
Midnight rain pattering gently down,
Leaves of the t'ung tree falling one by one
—These I hear in the echoing court.
I see you,
Your eyes ever bright
As the waves of the sea,
Your waist ever slender
As the willow tree,
Your hands ever beckoning
From the darkness to me.
Heartache to think of,
Regrets of the spring.
So with half-formed thoughts and bitterness
—Until at last the dawn creeps in.

SOUTH OF THE RIVER

Po Chü-i

Beautiful land south of the river,
Lovely landscape remembered so well
—Waters glowing crimson in the dawning,
In the spring flowing an indigo blue.
Soft, caressing breezes,
You are enshrined in my heart evermore.

THE PEACH BLOSSOMS OF TA LIN TEMPLE

Po Chü-i

When the fourth month has passed
And the fragrant flowers have fled,
The peach blossoms of Ta Lin Temple
Burst forth in profusion.
Long have I searched
For the secret home of spring
—But never did I dream to find it here!

UNDYING GRASS

Po Chü-i

The grass springs quickly,
Growing everywhere.
A single year is witness
To its splendor and decay.
Wild fires may assault it
But cannot all destroy,
And with the winds of spring
It burgeons forth again.
Its fragrance invades the ancient roads,
And with sunny days
It drapes ruined towns in green.
It speeds glad folk
Upon their way
And waves farewell
With lush and lavish hand.

THE CHARCOAL BURNER

Po Chü-i

Halfway up South Mountain
A gray-haired old man cuts wood,
Then converts it into charcoal.
His face is smeared with soot,
Dust, and smoke,
And black are his ten fingers.
He sells his charcoal,
But how much can he earn?
Just enough to find food
For his mouth
And clothes for his body.
A pity it is to see his rags,
A single garment without lining.
He worries about the price of charcoal
And hopes that cold weather may come.
With the night
Snow falls on the city
And lies a foot deep
At the coming of dawn.
He harnesses his ox to his cart
And breaks the ice from the ruts
As he goes.
The ox is weary,
The old man is hungry,
And when the sun is at its height,
They rest in the mud
Outside the gate of the south market.
Two young men ride up on horseback,
One handsomely dressed in yellow,

The other clad in a robe of white.
In their hands
They bear official dispatches
And proclaim the imperial commands.
The old man, hearing,
Shouts to the ox
And turns his cart to the north
—His charcoal has been seized by decree,
Taken for use in the palace,
All the thousand pounds of it,
The result of his labor,
And to lament would be of no avail.
See! This length of worthless ribbon,
Which he ties
To the head of his ox!
This, and this only
Is the reward of his toil.

REJECTED

Po Chü-i

My eyes are now dry,
Yet my gauze sleeve is still wet with tears.
Though the night
Is now far gone,
Revelry still fills the great hall
Of the palace.
I have not grown old,
Nor have my face or form lost their charm.
But already
Has my lord withdrawn his favor.
And I?
I bow before the incense bowl
And await
The coming of the dawn.

SPRING RAIN

Meng Hao Jan (689–740)

It is said of Meng Hao Jan that "he used to seek inspiration by riding on a donkey over the snow."

> Dreaming in the spring,
> I was not conscious of the dawning
> —And now I hear the birds singing
> All about.
> With the coming of the evening
> I listen to the sounds of wind and rain.
> Ah! Who knows how many blossoms
> May be falling?

THE NIGHT FERRY

Meng Hao Jan

Though it is after nightfall,
Travelers still seek
To cross the Hsiang River
By ferry.
In the dewy air
I recognize the fragrance
Of the russet pears
And hear the singing
Of the lotus gatherers.
The boatman steers
By the light
Of the fires on the shore;
The fisherboy sleeps
In the mist by the lake.
I hear strangers nearby asking,
"In which direction
Lies the town of Chen Yang?"

WAITING

Meng Hao Jan

The westering sun
Casts shadows on the hills.
The deep valleys lie gloomy and chill.
The moon
Climbs above the tops of the pines.
The breeze and the spring whisper clear.
The vapors rise.
A weary woodsman returns from his task.
The birds on the boughs
Have gone early to rest.
Though you promised
To pass the night here with me,
Still alone with my lute
On the green path I wait.

PEI MANG HILL

Shen Ch'üan Ch'i (d. 713)

Shen Ch'üan Ch'i was secretary of the Board of Rites.

On Pei Mang Hill
Over Lo Yang Town
The graves lie, row on row,
As they've lain autumns without number
Until now.
Down in the city
The bells chime out,
And songs resound.
On the hill
One hears but the wind
In the cedar and the pine.

NIGHT ON THE CHI PAN HILLS

Shen Ch'üan Ch'i

A solitary wanderer,
I have traveled a thousand li.
Tonight I rest high up
On the western peak of Chi Pan.
The moon has descended
And draws near my window.
The fresh scent of spring is everywhere,
And the cuckoo sounds his note.
My mind drifts here and there.
At dawn I seem to hear
The crowing of the rooster at Pao Chêng.

RETIRED

Shen Ch'üan Ch'i

I have retired,
Setting all affairs aside.
I lean on my staff, and from the height
I watch the farmers till their fields.
In the spring
The flowers, having ample moisture, flourish.
At times I go into the gloomy forest
To gather herbs.
Here, where the country is wild,
Men ask of each other their names,
And the very birds seem to do the same.
I come and go and find my pleasure alone.
I am ashamed to be here,
Shorn of the use of my abilities.

BEAUTY

Tz'ui Hu (eighth century)

Within this gate
On this same day last year
There appeared the face of a woman
That rivaled the loveliness
Of the peach.
Alas!
I know not
Whither the beautiful face has vanished,
For today
The blossoms of the peach
Laugh alone in the springtime breeze.

FIREFLIES IN THE MOONLIGHT

Li Ch'i (eighth century)

At times they draw close
To the curtain,
Then retreat afar
As if in fear of the screen.
They fly in the moonlight,
Then descend to the pool,
Where each and its reflection
Make two.

INSCRIPTION ON OLD WU'S HOUSE

Li Ch'i

Things remain,
But man passes away,
And we see him not again.
I leave my horse in the court.
(Alas! my sorrow is great.)
Before the window
The bamboo grows wild
On the neglected land,
And beyond the gate
The mountains loom green
As aforetime.
Sadly I raise my eyes
To the autumn sky
And hear the rustle
Of fallen leaves.
I see the old, gnarled, withered willows,
Where perch chilled owls.
My thoughts turn to you,
And my tears flow
As do the waters to the east.
For whom
Year after year henceforth
Will the blossoms open?

ON SEEING TSENG CHANG YÜN DANCING

Yang Kuei Pei (eighth century)

Yang Kuei Pei, one of the most famous women in Chinese history, was the concubine of the emperor Hsüan Tsung (Ming Huang, of the T'ang Dynasty, the patron of Chinese drama). Her family so dominated state affairs that finally the army revolted and demanded her execution. Many stories and poems have been inspired by the events of her life.

Her gauze sleeve
Gives forth perfume
At every step.
She is like unto a crimson lotus
Trembling on its stem
In the autumn breeze,
A light cloud wafted by a gentle wind,
A tender branch
Of the weeping willow
Swaying at the pool's edge,
Just kissing the surface
Of the water.

OLD SONGS

Liu Ch'ang Ch'ing (eighth century)

Harmonious,
Full of harmony
Is the seven-stringed lute,
And soft-voiced
Is the cool breeze in the pines.
Though you may yourself
Love the songs of old time,
There are few
Who will play them today.

A VISIT TO NAN CHI

Liu Ch'ang Ch'ing

My wooden sandals leave their imprint
In the green moss
As I make my way along the path.
The white clouds trail peacefully in the sky.
The recent rain seems
To have endued the pines with new color.
I follow the flower-bordered stream
To its course in the hills.
The doorway to the hut is closed
With a screen woven of sweet grass.
We sit facing each other in contemplation,
Forgetful of speech.

THE OLD SOLDIER

Liu Ch'ang Ch'ing

He led great armies against the south
And in his time
Subdued countless thousands
And drove them into flight.
Now, relieved of his command,
Weary and sad,
His country has need of him no more.
Old, almost alone he stands,
Dreaming of his days of glory,
When he and his good sword were one.
Oh, how many, how vast
Are the rivers of Han!
Who knows
Where the sun of his life will set,
And when and how he will go?

RETURNING FROM THE DAY'S LABOR

Liu Ch'ang Ch'ing

The day looms dark
Over the far-off mountains.
Under the stormy sky
The houses of the poor are white
In the winter's blast.
A dog barks before the brushwood gate.
Piercing wind and whirling snow
Greet us
On our return at night.

MOTHER AND SON

Meng Chiao (751–814)

The tender mother
With her thread and needle
Sews clothing for her son
About to leave his home.
Her work is fine—
Oh, so fine!
And all the while
She has the fearful thought
That it may be long, long
Before his return.
Who says
That a mother's heart
Is as barren grass
—Or even that three springs
Can ever compensate?

SELF-IMMOLATION

Meng Chiao

The yu túng trees grow old together,
And mandarin ducks do not survive alone.
When the husband dies,
The loyal wife should be buried with him;
For thus to sacrifice one's self
Is the way of life.[1]
Within me there is no fear or shrinking,
For my love is profound
As the deepest well.

[1] Suicide has been very common among the Chinese. Suttee, treated in this poem, had quasi-government recognition in Fukien Province.

COMING DOWN SUNG SHAN

Sung Chih Wei (d. 710)

Sung Chih Wei was a T'ang official, banished for corrupt practices and forced to commit suicide. Sung Shan was one of the sacred mountains of the Buddhists.

Hand in hand with my beloved
I came slowly down Sung Shan.
The moon, shining brightly on us
Through the pines,
Brought long, long thoughts.
Yon moon will shine as bright
Throughout years without number,
But you, my love,
When will you walk with me again?

THE OLD FISHERMAN

Liu Tsung Yüan (773–810)

The old fisherman passed the night
On the West Rock of the River Hsiang.
At dawn he drew pure water from a well
And cooked his meal
Over a fire of sh'u bamboo.
The mist vanished, and the sun arose,
· But no human was in sight.
His oars made the only sound,
And as he rowed,
He looked out on the stream
And upon the green hills.
Then, after gazing intently
Into the blue sky
He steered in midstream
—And again watched the clouds
Drifting lazily, far up, beyond the cliff.

NOSTALGIA

Li Ts'an Hsü (d. 925)

Li Ts'an Hsü was the first emperor of the Later T'ang Dynasty. He was murdered by an actor to whom he had given an important post.

I seem to remember
That once, in a deep peach-shaded glen
We feasted, danced and sang
—Then tears were our companions
As we left the gates.
Was it all a dream, naught but a dream
Of waning moon and falling blossoms
In a mist?

THE MOON AND MAN

Wang Chien (d. 918)

After a wild youth Wang Chien became a wise statesman
and was later created prince of the state of Shu. He served
as a provincial governor for eight years.

In the courtyard
Where the crows nest in the trees,
The earth gleams white,
The dew forms silently,
And the blossoms of the cassia tree
Are damp.
Men look up
At the brilliant moon,
But none can know
In what man's house
The sadness of autumn dwells.

RUINS

Wang Chien

The ruined palace
Lies in utter desolation.
The very flowers
Seem to fade and fall in silence.
Some withered white-haired crones
Still linger and idly chatter,
Talking of mysterious and ancient kings.

THE RUINED PALACE

Wang Chien

The green hills encompass the ancient palace.
The Jade Tower lies prostrate;
The ornate halls are empty.
The warrior emperor is no more.
And now the caprices of the wild flowers
And the yellow butterflies
Dictate to spring.

THE MONASTERY AT PO SHAN

Ch'ang Chien (eighth century)

Ch'ang Chien was a Taoist recluse.

> I arrive at the ancient shrine
> At early morn,
> Just as the sun
> Has touched the treetops.
> I enter the hall of meditation
> By a shady winding path
> Amid the flowers and the trees.
> Among the hills
> The birds rejoice,
> And man's heart is free from shadows
> As this pool.
> Here all worldly sounds are hushed,
> Save the sweet chime
> Of the monastery bell.

VAIN ENDEAVOR

Hsi Feng (ninth century)

On the six roads of the city
When the morning guns boom out,
On foot, on horseback,
On rolling wheels
From all directions
Masters and servants alike stream forth
At the urge of food and wealth,
And every class of folk
Meets on the road.
The year's events
Flow like the waters of a stream,
Then, most concerned with mundane things alone
Soon fade, and are forgotten
Like the blossoms
Fallen in the winds
Of yesterdawn.
Alas! Gain and fame grant no repose to man,
And he realizes not
That the triumph of today
Will be tomorrow
As vain
As that of yesterday.

THE SONG OF LUNG HSI

Ch'en T'ao (ninth century)

After serving as an astronomer under the later T'angs Ch'en T'ao retired and, with his wife, also a scholar, raised oranges for a livelihood. He was a strong antimilitarist.

> They had sworn
> To sweep the Hsiung Nu[1]
> From the face of the earth,
> With no thought
> Of the risk to their own lives.
> And now full five thousand warriors
> In fur-trimmed garb
> Have died on Tartar soil.
> Their bones lie grim
> On Wu T'ing's banks,
> But in the spring
> The dead men still live on
> In the dreams of their widowed wives.

[1] The people of western Mongolia, ancestors of the Huns and the Turks.

THE WARRIOR

Wang Ch'ang Ling (eighth century)

The fighting has ceased.
Seated in his jade-white saddle
On his warhorse Liu,
The warrior rides homeward
From the field of battle
Beneath the wintry sun.
The vibrations
Of the iron war drum
Still fill his ear,
And the blood
On his sheathed sword
Is not yet dry.

YELLOW SUNSET

Wang Ch'ang Ling

The beacon burns in the West City
On the Pai Ch'ih Tower;
The wind blows in from the sea.
I sit alone
In the yellow autumn sunset
And watch the moon rise
Over the mountain pass.
Homesick, I play upon my flute,
And ten thousand sadnesses creep over me
As I dream of my homeland
—And of you.

AMBITION

Wang Ch'ang Ling

While the young wife tarried
In her apartments,
Sadness did not seem to touch her.
But when, one spring day,
Arrayed in gayest garments,
She stepped out on her tower
And saw the stir of life
In the slim young green willow branches,
Regret swept over her
That she had urged her husband
To depart to seek high office.

THE TRADER

Liu Chia (ninth century)

The trader prepares for his journey
By lamplight,
Saying, "I am already late
In my starting,
And must make haste,
For there are perilous paths
In the mountains."
Meanwhile, cruel bandits,
Savage as wild beasts,
Lie in ambush at the roadside.
They pursue, overtake
And encounter the trader.
His gold and gems are looted,
Carried off to the four winds,
His empty bags left lying,
Abandoned at the crossroads.

In Yangchew stands his stately home,
But his bones lie white, unburied.
On that day
His young wife, all unknowing,
Sits before her mirror,
Toying with a branch
Of bright blossoms.

GLORY

Ts'ao Sung (ninth century)

Ah!
Picture a fertile land,
Its mountains and rivers,
When war invades its frontiers!
And the people?
How can they exist,
How find their livelihood,
Or ever be restored again?
Talk not to me
Of such things
Where a man wins fame
By heaping up
Ten thousand dry human bones.

A SONG FROM EXILE

Li Yü (937–78)

Li Yü was the name assumed by Nan T'ang Chu, last em-
peror of the Southern T'ang Dynasty. He was more inter-
ested in pleasure and in poetry than in affairs of state. He
died miserably in exile in 975, reportedly by poison.

> Flowers of spring,
> Moons of autumn,
> When will you ever cease?
> —And of the past
> What can you know?
> Last night
> In the bright moonlight,
> When the east wind sighed
> About my room,
> I dared not think of my homeland,
> Whither I cannot return.

THE TRYST

Li Yü (937–78)

Bright flowers, the dark of the moon,
And thick mist for concealment.
This is a propitious time
To go to her lover.
She removes her stockings
And walks down the fragrant path,
Carrying her gold-embroidered slippers
In her hand.
At the south side of the painted hall
She sees him and, trembling,
Embraces him, whispering,
"Ah, it is difficult
Thus to meet and then leave you.
Take me, I entreat you,
And follow the dictates of your love."

VAIN REGRETS

Li Yü

Withered are the forest flowers.
The strength of spring has all too swiftly passed.
How could it be otherwise
With cold rains at dawn and storms at eventide?
A dainty face, rouged and powdered,
With tear-stained cheeks,
A young man distraught with love
—These momentous hours of life,
Will they ever return?
The waters flow unceasing to the east,
But suffering and grief abide.

I REMEMBER, I REMEMBER

Li Yü

Idle dreams
Of the faraway southland,
Just as it blooms fragrant in the spring.
Strains of music
From a boat on a green river.
Catkin dust filling the city's streets.
Folk eagerly awaiting the awakening of the flowers.

Idle dreams
Of the faraway southland,
Just as clear autumn appears.
A thousand-li sweep of river and mountain,
Lightly touched by the season's chill hues.
Down in the stream by the rushes
A single small boat lies moored.
High in some moonlit tower
The notes of a flute are heard.

LOOKING BACKWARD

Li Yü

How can man avoid suffering,
In this, our transient life?
I am a soul, alone,
With no limit to my sorrow.
In a dream I am transported
Back to my native land
—And when I awake,
Straightway my eyes are filled with tears.
Who is here
To climb the lofty tower with me,
To look out afar, as once we did,
On a clear, bright autumn day?
Ah! days that are past
—And I myself am empty,
As though I move and live within a dream.

AN IDYL

Li Yü

High-pitched notes
From the copper reeds in the bamboo flute.
The slender, jadelike fingers
Draw forth music sweet,
Slow new measures that move them to their depth.
Each reads the other's eyes
Then both are swept away by passion's surging wave.
Now rain and clouds are mingled
Behind the brocade screen,
And the longed-for harmony
Unites the two as one.
But no sooner is the feast consumed
Than keen hunger calls once more,
And the dream of love now merges
With the gentle rain of spring.

THOUGHTS AT DAYBREAK

Li Yü

It is early dawn.
The moon is setting,
And the thin morning mist begins to lift.
I toss and turn on my pillow
Between fitful sleeping and waking.
My dreams are of fragrant plants
That cling so tightly to the life they love.
From high in the heavens the wild geese call.
Orioles twitter—then scatter.
The blossoms fall
And lie in disarray.
The painted hall is desolate and silent.
Do not sweep away the crimson petals.
Leave them,
That they may rejoice the dancers
When they return to their repose.

THE DEPOSED EMPEROR

Li Yü

For forty years I dwelt in my homeland
—Three thousand li of plain and hill and river,
With its Phoenix Hall and Dragon Tower
Soaring even to the heavens.
There I had trees of jade with coral boughs
That spread their mistlike shade.
Never once, in all those years
Recked I of arms or war.
But a morning came
When I found myself a captive and a slave.
My back became bowed
Like that of Shen,
My hair white, like that of P'ang.
These witness to my fate.
I suffered most when I departed
From the sacred temple court,
Where music rang and songs were chanted
In farewell.
Then, as I faced the palace women,
I wept.

SPRING MORNING

Li Shang Yin (813–58)

The dawn is clear
With but little dew
And a gentle breeze.
Alone I arise and draw my curtain.
An oriole sings,
And the flowers smile.
For whom, after all,
Is the spring here,
If not for me?

HEARTLESS SPRING

Li Shang Yin

The last guest has departed
From the high hall.
In the small garden
The blossoms, caught up by the wind,
Whirl in confusion along the winding paths,
Catching the light here and there
As they go.
No one can sweep up the broken pieces
Of my heart.
Grief pierces my eyes.
All the gifts of my love
Did I give unto spring
—And what have I left?
Only a tear-drenched sleeve.

EVENTIDE

Li Shang Yin

The sun is descending
Toward its western cave.
I seek out the hermit priest
In his thatched hut.
Where is he,
Now that the leaves have fallen?
My path has led me through the hills
Where the clouds are lowering.
Alone I strike the first evening chimes
And lean against a bough of the climbing vine.
I lose myself in reverie.
What a tiny being am I
In this great world!
Have I need of either love or hate?

TO THE PEAR TREE AT THE LEFT OF MY DOOR

Ch'iu Wei (ninth century)

Your cold beauty
Outrivals quite
The pure snow.
Your fragrance becomes part of our robes,
And the wandering breezes of spring
Will waft the scent
Even to the palace of the king.

THE WEAVER

Ch'ien Ch'i (eighth century)

The Milky Way is clearly seen
As frost or jade.
The north wind sweeps away the fragrance of the lotus.
By the light of a solitary lamp
A young wife weaves.
Restraining her loneliness,
She wipes away her frequent tears
As the water clock drips out
The endless hours of the night.
The thin clouds obscure the moon above the eaves.
A bird calls from his roost,
And the geese rise in flight.
Whose wife is she
Who weaves a lovebird on her loom?
An embroidered curtain hangs before her sleeping room.
Through her open window
She hears the falling leaves.
Pity her,
Who so softly mourns her absent lord.

THE EMPTY CAGE

Lu Kuei Meng (ninth century)

Lu Kuei Meng was an eccentric whose great joy was to go about in a small boat with fishing tackle, a portable stove for making tea, and some books.

> I have cared for you for many years.
> Now I find your cage door open,
> And you have disappeared.
> Sad at heart
> I search for you,
> With alas, but little hope!
> You are likely
> Down by some autumn stream
> Among the flowers and reeds,
> Where the bright moon shines.

INSPIRATION

Wei Ying Wu (eighth century)

Wei Ying Wu rose from being a bodyguard of the emperor
Ming Huang to the governorship of Soochow.

After nine days of labor
I was free again
And rode off to your home.
Though you were not there,
My visit was not in vain.
At seeing the stream
That flows before your gateway
And the snow piled high upon your hills,
My whole being was strangely inspired
To write verse.

TO A HERMIT

Wei Ying Wu

I hum a tune as I walk abroad
On this cold autumn night
—And my thoughts turn toward you.
All is silent on the bare mountain,
Save a thud now and then
As a pine cone falls.
As with me,
Sleep has not yet come to you.

GOLD

Chang Wei (eighth century)

In this world
Friendship too often is measured
In yellow gold.
Without increase of yellow gold
There may be union for a space,
But in the end the two will separate,
Each following the dictates
Of his own heart.

AUTUMN MOON

Tu Shen Yen (seventh and eighth centuries)

Tu Shen Yen was the grandfather of Tu Fu. He served as architect in the Imperial Academy.

I sit alone and look out into the night.
The moon rides high in autumn's sky.
Now a crescent bow,
It will open soon to full circle
Like a fan.
Dews, sad as tears, have often bathed
The clear orb's light.
It is darkened now by a wind-blown shadow,
And my gauze garment is pierced by the cold air.
I bow my head,
And find it bitter
To bid farewell to departing friends.

ON MEETING A MOUNTED COURIER
ON HIS WAY TO THE CAPITAL

Ts'en Ts'an (eighth century)

Ts'en Ts'an was a censor under the T'ang emperor Su Tsung and was later governor of Chia Chou, far from his home.

> My old garden
> Is far, far away
> On the road to the east.
> My long sleeves
> Do not suffice
> To dry my tears.
> Since you are on horseback,
> Neither paper nor brush
> Is at hand.
> I pray you,
> Convey just this message for me:
> "All is well. I am safe."

LIANG'S OLD GARDEN

Ts'en Ts'an

At eve
In Liang's old garden
The crows fly to and fro.
Though a few houses may still stand,
All else is bleak and sad.
The trees behind the courtyard wall
Do not know that all have fled,
And with the coming of spring
They burst into bloom
As in the days
That are gone and dead.

AN INVITATION

Ting Hsien Chih (eighth century)

Ting Hsien Chih was an official under the T'ang Dynasty.

The sun rising red over the mountains
Aroused me from sleep
—And I saw that spring had arrived.
A robin and a white-throated bird
Were fluttering about the highest eaves,
Singing their songs,
But they would not enter in.
At the booming of the morning drum I look outside.
The courtyard is a cloud of cherry blossoms,
And the peach trees
Have brightened my tower and balcony
With their color.
I have bought a bargeload of the finest food;
It is the second month,
When all the people celebrate.
I await your coming,
That you may fill your cup with me,
To hail the moon in choicest wine,
To toast it as it waxes and wanes,
Then waxes and wanes yet once again.

HAVOC

Chang Chi (eighth century)

Chang Chi was a tutor in the Imperial Academy.

Last year we were fighting the Yüeh Chi Tartars
On the northern frontier.
Before the city not a single company
Remained unscathed.
We had no news of the soldiers of Han
Nor of the wild western foe
—We were cut off from the living and the dead.
The tents lay abandoned
—Not a man to salvage them.
Riderless horses galloped back
And stood untended by their standards.
I abstained from offering sacrifice
To your spirit,
For I knew not
Whether you were of the living or the slain.
Alas! the whole canopy of high heaven
Re-echoes with the weeping
Brought on by this unhappy war.

THE MIDNIGHT BELL

Chang Chi

The moon is low in the sky.
The dew gathers.
Now and then the silence is broken
By the call of a bird.
The fishermen's fires
Cast the shadows of the maples
On the shore.
From Han Shan Temple, beyond ancient Soochow
The midnight bell rings out.
The travelers in their boat
Stir in their sleep
At the gloomy, echoing sound.

AWAITING THE SWALLOWS

Chang Hsieh

I stood musing
High on the battlemented tower,
Watching in vain for the return of the swallows.
In the distance
Was a green-clad hill,
Down by a ford of the river.
Overhead were rosy clouds
That seemed to turn aside the rain.
Crows hopped and called,
And in the darkening sky
Hung a sickly yellow moon.

NEW YEAR'S THOUGHTS IN CAMP

Chang Shuo

Last year at Ching Nan
The plum blossoms lay as billowing drifts of snow.
This year at Chi Pai
The snow lies like great clouds
Of the blossoms of the plum.
All this saddens me,
To think that man's affairs
Thus swing back and forth, to and fro.
Yet I rejoice that the flowers
That ever depart with the dying year
Always return again.
Here the soldiers who guard the north frontier
Sing their songs the whole night long,
While over the city the sky glows red
With signal flares.
Far in the distance lies the great city of Chang An.
Would that I might stand upon its South Hill
And salute it in good wine!

MY COUNTRY HOME

Chu Kuang-i

On my farm
I have planted a hundred mulberry trees—and more,
And thirty mou of land
Are sown in millet.
Of food and raiment there is abundance
—Plenty to share with my friends.
In summer I harvest ku mi rice,
In autumn I drink chrysanthemum-flavored wine.
My wife has joy
In welcoming our guests.
I have an ever-obedient son.
In the evenings
I find pleasure in my garden
—And even if I drink too much,
I still can stagger home.
Everywhere is shade of elm and willow,
And in the summer
Cooling breezes come
Through my lattice window and my open door.
With ease
I see the Milky Way,
And the Great Bear when it is high or low.
I count my jars of wine still unopened.
Will you not come tomorrow
And make merry with me?

A LEAF FALLS

Hsieh Neng

Lightly a single leaf drifts slowly down.
Borne on the breeze,
It glides like a shadow and comes to earth.
What tree has sent forth
This first sign of autumn?
Its color has changed!
Yellow must be nigh,
Though the forest still stands green.
Alone the leaf floats
On the bosom of some clear stream
Or lies unseen on the pass.
To behold it brings sadness,
For the falling will not end with this one leaf.
The traveler's heart is as an empty moon.
Who would willingly seek out a new sorrow?

THE LUTE

Hsü An Chen

The hour was late,
And the Bushel Basket[1] lay low in the heavens.
Sad at heart I was gazing upon the moon,
When suddenly, from out the women's chamber
Of my neighbor's house,
Came the sound of a lute, with song,
Bringing sweet music to my ear.
As in my mind I saw her moth eyebrows
And seemed to see her jadelike fingers
Weave the melody.
Sudden desire seized upon me.
But her door was closed,
Fastened tightly with a silver lock.
Though I could hear her voice so near,
I knew she would not open,
I cannot sleep
—But I can dream of the maid within.

[1] The Great Bear.

THE DESERTED CITY OF SHIH TOU

Lin Yu Hsi

The city, walled in by mountains,
Stands desolate.
The ebbing tide
Reveals the solitary ruins.
The moon that crosses the River Huai
To climb the eastern towers
Still comes in the dead of night
To peer inside its battlements.

HSI SHIH

Lou Ying

When Hsi Shih was wont
To dye her yarn beside the stream,
On that same day she destroyed the hearts
Of men,
As she would the green moss upon the stone.
Now that she has departed
For Ku Su,
Never to return,
Will the peach and plum trees
On the bank
Blossom in the spring?

FAREWELL BY THE RIVER

Wang Po (648–76)

Wang Po was reputed to have written his best poems when
intoxicated.

It is early autumn.
At dawn I have come to meet
And bid farewell to my friend
At the teahouse by the river.
The bright moon seems to float
Upon the water.
I grieve, fearing that he has already set forth
Upon the stream.
When next I look,
The ferry is hidden by the trees
—And he has vanished.

THE TRAVELER

Wei Ch'ang Ching

The traveler's heart vies
With the sun and the moon,
Counting already
The time of his arrival
At his home.
The wind of autumn
Does not tarry for him,
But is at Lo Yang City
Before him.

VIEW FROM THE TOWER

Yang Shih Ngo

The artemesia and the flowers of the huai trees
Surround the town.
The hissing of the night rain from the hills
But increases the roar of the river.
The autumn wind
Has driven all carts and horses
From the marketplace.
Alone on the high tower
I reflect on the fate of kingdoms
Long since dead.

MY LADY'S GARDEN

Wang Piao

How early spring comes to your garden!
Your plants are already laden with flowers.
Like guardians they laugh at your approach,
And their fragrance settles
On your lovely hair.
The earth welcomes you
And rejoices to be near you.
Heaven gives bountifully of its rain and dew.
Butterflies come dancing
In the bright light about you.
At eventide
The birds fly joyously to your tower.
I wish I could rise to you as a cloud.
My heart opens to you as to the sun.
What place does not seem dark
Compared to the peach and plum trees
By your door!

SPRING MOUNTAIN

Yü Liang Shih

Spring Mountain surpasses all
In beauty.
I am held in its thrall
So that I forget to depart
When dusk comes down.
The water that I hold
In the hollow of my hand
Reflects the moon.
The flowers are so fragrant
That their scent
Penetrates my robes.
Though I am in the mood for verse,
The lines refuse to come.
When I would fain take my leave,
Its sweet charm draws me back.
When I look to the south
To learn
Whence come the chimes I hear,
I see a tiny bell tower
Half-concealed in a sea of green.

GRASS

Chen Shan Min (Sung Dynasty)

The grass may wither,
But its roots live on.
And when spring returns,
It blossoms once again.
But my sorrow arises within my heart,
And spring brings no blossoms
Back to me.

MEMORIES

Ching Kai (Sung Dynasty)

Dreams of the heart long past
Bring shyness and sighs
To the inner eye.
How often we walked together
In our fine garments
On the peach-shaded bank of the river!
How often we met, fans in hand,
In the almond-blossom-scented old tea house!
Ah, what regrets!
Who could know
That spring winds would so soon cease to blow?
Who could guess
That light morning clouds could vanish
Thus quickly?
Heaven itself grows old
When love gives place to hate.
Bees gathering the sweet
Understand not the bitter,
Nor can swallows know aught
Of man's grief.
Loves of the past are with us ever.
On what day can they die?

ON THE MOUNTAIN

Chen Yü-i (Sung Dynasty)

On the bare mountain
I hear the ring of a woodsman's ax.
High on a ridge is a dwelling.
The sun glints on a pool.
The woods are bright.
The stream reflects the light,
And the flowers dance in the breeze.

THE DEAD PAST

Chu Tun Yu (Southern Sung Dynasty)

Often I admired the plum blossoms
Until I was drunk with wine,
And to please fair women
I wrote verses in scarlet ink
On silken sashes and bridal scarves,
While they served me strong drink
In kingfisher cups as my reward.
Now I am old, and all is changed.
When I would salute the flowers with wine,
My tears fall and moisten my robe,
And I desire but to close my door and sleep.
Nor do I longer care
What patterns
The falling plum blossoms
Trace upon the snow.

MY COUNTRY

Yueh Fei (1102–41)

Yueh Fei was a famous Sung general.

From afar
I look upon China, my fatherland.
I behold many cities and walls;
I recall the green willows and blossoms
That encircled and adorned Dragon Pavilion
And Phoenix Tower,
And the Hill of Ten Thousand Years.
All are now weed-grown, neglected,
With shards scattered everywhere.
Where once were the music of sheng and song
One sees but the tracks
Of evil men and iron-shod hoofs.
The watercourses and moats are choked
With the bodies of my people.
Our soldiers lie transpierced
With spear and with sword.
Lamenting is heard on mountain and stream,
And a thousand hamlets stand deserted and silent.
Oh, when can I rally a valiant host
To cross the clear river
And crush the Mongol foe,
To free my people and the land of my fathers?
Then would I be content to mount the yellow crane on
  high.[1]

[1] To die.

THE CREATOR

Liu K'o Chuang (1187–1269)

Leaf after leaf, light as a butterfly's wing,
Bit after bit of red, even in tiny dots.
There are folk who say
That the Lord, creator of all these things,
Has no compassion
On the hundred kinds of leaf and flower.
In the morning one sees the treetops,
Laden heavy with green leaves,
And at eventide they have vanished from the bough.
There are folk who say
That the Lord, creator of all these things,
Truly loves the leaves and flowers,
Though the rain has stripped them,
And the wind has carried them away.

CONCEALMENT

Hsin Ch'i (d. 1198)

Hsin Ch'i was a statesman under two emperors of the Sung Dynasty. He is famous for his remark that there were only three things worthwhile in life—to drink, to travel, and to sleep.

When my years
Were few in number
And I knew not
The taste of grief,
I wrote what I thought
Were songs of grief
—I, to whom sadness was unknown.
Now I have tasted sorrow,
Drunk of sorrow to the full,
But when I wish to speak of sorrow,
Of deep and heartfelt grief,
I prate instead
Of the autumn weather,
And of the fine cool days
It has brought.

FLEETING BLOSSOMS

Hsü Fu (eleventh century)

Hsü Fu was a native of Shansi Province, noted for his filial
piety. He did not marry until he was forty, for fear that his
wife would fail in her duty to his mother. Then, when his
mother died, he married. He was deaf, and people com-
municated with him by writing on the ground.

Yesterday they were crimson on the branch,
So fresh
That they stained my fingers at a touch.
This morning I searched for them in vain.
For they had already vanished
And lay
At the bottom of the pool.

STRUGGLE

Tai Fu Ku (twelfth century)

At midnight
Man's restlessness does cease.
At the fifth hour
A hundred dreams are scattered.
And at cockcrow
Sleep departs from ten thousand pillows.
A hundred quarter-hours
Is each day allotted,
But of these
Too few can man count his own.
When at night he seeks slumber,
His dreams exhaust him.
The clever and the rich
Dream that their wealth has flown,
And he who has succeeded
Imagines spirits all about him.
Since even in our sleep
We are pursued by haste and struggle,
Life grants us
But small time
For pure joy.

A SUMMER NIGHT

Yang Wan Li (1124–1206)

Yang Wan Li was keeper of the Imperial library.

> The heat of the night differs but little
> From that of high noon.
> I open the door and stand a while,
> Bathed in the bright rays of the moon.
> Here in the shade,
> Where the bamboo and trees grow thick,
> The insects sing,
> And though there is but little wind,
> The air is cool.

THE MORNING FERRY

Yang Wan Li

Through the mist
The river and the mountains are dimly seen,
And from the crowing of the roosters
And the barking of the dogs
I would surmise that we are passing a village.
The little ferry has a coat of thick frost;
And when I set my foot upon a board,
My shoe leaves its perfect print upon it.

EVENING AT WILLOW BRIDGE

Lu Yu (1125–1209)

Lu Yu was a historian of note.

> As I watch in the tangled wood
> For the crane's return,
> I hear a fish leap in the tiny stream.
> The passing clouds bear no threat of rain
> But float across the green mountainside.

BLOSSOMTIME

Lu Yu

I love the familiar flowers
With a madness close unto death.
I only fear that their beauty and fragrance
Will be injured by the hot sun and wind.
Would that I could send a petition
To the Bright Palace in the sky
To plead
That we might borrow spring's sunshade,
To protect the plants we love!

THE FISHERMAN AND THE POET

Lu Yu

The fisherman's thatched hut stands
On the riverbank among the mallows
Like a picture.
The green mountains loom before his door.
The mists trail over the stream,
And the rain falls softly
As the old man guides his boat
Through the waves to catch his fish.
Alas! His parents were unlettered,
And he can neither read nor write
—Nor does the beauty of the scene before him
Mean a single line to him.
And I?
Though a poet, I am old and full of shame
That the power has departed from my brush.
Looking out upon the mountain and the river
I heave three sighs, in vain!

THE BIRTH OF AUTUMN

Liu Lin (1241–93)

Yestermorn
I witnessed the birth of autumn
In a single leaf.
Today a thousand cliffs
And ten thousand folded valleys are clear and bright.
I would summon the western wind
To heal this illness in my bones.
So at dawn I sit upon a stone
And hearken to its whisper
In the pines.

THE LIFE OF A FARMER

Chao Meng Fu (1254–1322)

Chao Meng Fu was a lineal descendant of the first Sung emperor, Secretary of the Board of War, a poet, and a painter. His wife was also an artist.

Let me tell you of the life of a farmer.
It is a bitter one,
Spent in a field of weeds and water.
The red sun beats down upon his back
Until it is nearly split open.
His sweat pours forth like rain.
He crawls on hands and knees in waist-deep water.
The new shoots spring up,
Sharp as double-edged swords.
How painful is the suffering of his flesh!
He tills the field,
And his wife carries food to him,
Just when the noonday sun is at its height.
He has not a minute to rest from his labor
Or to escape the sun.
Yet who gives thought
To the food of the common people,
Though none of the grains is obtained without labor?
I tell this to reveal the toil of the farmer
And to prove
That idleness has never been preached,
Even in olden days.

THE WANDERER

Liu Chi (1311–75)

Liu Chi was instrumental in driving out the Mongols (of
the Yüan Dynasty). He was at first a confidant of the em-
peror, but was later poisoned at the instance of new fa-
vorites, who replaced him.

In my youthful years I traveled far
And wandered to the remote four corners
Of the world.
Heaven and earth are spread so wide
That mountains and rivers have their place
In endless space.
A multitude of birds fly in perfect freedom,
And tall and hoary trees stand wide and cool.
Climbing high, my eye takes in
Ten thousand li of land.
Thinking of ancient times,
My heart is touched with sadness.
As I stand alone and watch the floating clouds
I wonder why I, too, cannot soar
And move as they,
Driven forward by the wind!

THE THUNDERSTORM

Wang Yang Ming (1472–1528)

Wang Yang Ming was a late Confucian philosopher. He occupied many high civil and military posts, including provincial governorships.

Last night I lodged
At the mountain's topmost peak.
The moon was gloriously bright,
But in the darkness
I heard the crash of thunder
At the mountain's base.
With daybreak came some climbers from below.
Upon my inquiry
They told of a violent storm of wind and rain
Which had struck in the third watch
Of the night
And left their thatched hut in ruins.

EARLY SPRING

Wei Chuang (tenth century)

Wei Chuang was a miser, of whom it was said that he counted the grains of rice that he ate and weighed the firewood for cooking it.

> An oriole is singing,
> So dawn must be near.
> Though the door is still closed,
> I sense that the fine weather has come.
> Through my window
> One clear ray of the moon enters
> And visits my pillow.

THE TRUANT

Cheng Hao (1032–1107)

That noon
The clouds were as fleece,
And the breeze was gentle.
I wandered happy
By the river,
Finding delight
In the trees and the flowers.
Those who saw me,
Not knowing the pure joy
In my heart,
Looked upon me
As they would
A young truant from school.

RANDOM THOUGHTS

Cheng Hao

When freed from the worldly cares of living,
Reflection and contemplation come.
Awakening, I see the sun
Glow red through my eastern casement,
And ten thousand diverse ideas
Swim through my mind.
In peace and quiet, well content with the joys
The four seasons bring,
The path of my reveries ranges far
—Beyond the earth, even unto the heavens.
It enters the wind
And revolves inside the clouds.
With clear vision I know
That he who is not debauched by wealth or honors,
Whom poverty or the low and mean in life
Can never stain
—This one is worthy to be called the son of man;
He is of heroic mould.

THE FEAST OF LANTERNS

Ou Yang Hsiu (1007–72)

Ou Yang Hsiu was vice-president of the Board of Rites and was a renowned historian, poet, and essayist.

At last year's Feast of Lanterns
The moon in the willows
Joined with the lights
To make the flower market
Bright as day.
And there
In the failing twilight
My love and I did meet.
At this year's Feast of Lanterns
Moon and lanterns
Gave light as before,
But my love, alas,
Is not with me,
And the sleeve of my spring gown
Is wet with tears.

PEACE OF MIND

Shao Yao (1011–77)

Though the waters may flow tempestuously,
Here I am at rest.
Though the flowers never cease to fall,
I find peace within my heart.
I am not like those men
Caught up in the fever and turmoil
Of worldly affairs.
Theirs is no breadth of vision,
Nor do they know aught
Of the true values of life.

WAKEFUL

Su Tung Po (1036–1101)

Su Tung Po (Su Shih), a poet of the first rank, was president of the Board of Rites and a member of the Han Lin Academy. In 1073 he built a hut on the eastern slope of a hill and thereafter assumed the name Su Tung Po (Su of the Eastern Slope).

My neighbor in the east
Owns many aspen trees.
It is autumn.
I lie alone under my window.
I cannot sleep
But listen to the sound of the driving rain
And watch the insects
Hover around my lamp.

FLOWER SHADOWS

Su Tung Po

In rows and heaps
The blossoms crowd
Upon the jade-green terrace.
Several times have I summoned my boy
To sweep them away.
His efforts have had but small success,
For no sooner does the sunset
Carry them off
Than the bright moon,
Rising,
Gathers and brings them again.

CAMPAIGNING

Na Lan Hsing Te (1655–85)

Na Lan Hsing Te was an officer in the Manchu Guards,
hopelessly in love with an imperial concubine.

A march through the mountains,
A march along the streams on the high frontier
Toward the Pass of Yü Kwan.[1]
In the deep darkness glow a thousand lights
In the tents of the army.
A night watch in the wind,
A night watch in the snow,
A clamor that breaks into sleep
And into happy dreams of my home.
I know an old garden
Where such sounds are not heard.

[1] Yü Kwan Pass is near Shanhaikwan (Linyu), on the Great Wall.

DROUGHT

Yüan Chiu Ts'ai (eighteenth century)

A long time has passed
Since heaven saw fit
To send us rain.
I call my boy
To draw water
From the depths of the well
And moisten my garden.
Even though it be but the strength
Of a cupful of water,
It reveals the compassion
In my heart
For the flowers.

A WARM INVITATION

Yüan Chiu Ts'ai

Do not laugh at my tower
Because it is high.
Its height is most useful to me,
For I can see you coming
More than a li away.
Do not come in a cart,
For the noise of a cart
Frightens my birds away.
Do not come riding a horse,
For your horse eats my grass.
Do not come at sunrise,
For I loathe rising at dawn.
Do not come at twilight,
For at sunset
All my flowers are asleep.

THE SIMPLE LIFE

Yüan Chiu Ts'ai

I brought no public honors
With me at my birth.
I acquired them through merit
As I advanced.
Now I have tasted them
And can return
To the simple life.
Whenever I behold flowers,
I want to go back
To my home.
Why should I await
The end of spring
When I see the white clouds
Wander hither and thither
Without purpose,
Through the empty sky?

THE WHEELBARROW

Ch'eng Tzu Lung (seventeenth century)

Ch'eng Tzu Lung was an official under the last Ming emperor. He retired and became a Buddhist priest. Later, involved in a revolutionary plot, he was captured and committed suicide.

The wheelbarrow goes "pan, pan"
At twilight in the yellow dust,
The husband pushing from behind,
The wife straining on a rope at the wheel.
They have abandoned their home
But know not where to turn.
Their food has been naught
But the seeds of the green elm tree,
And they seek a happier place
Where they might find better food
—Even thin rice gruel—
To sustain their lives.
As they move
Through the yellow wormwood patch,
They perceive a house ahead.
With the hope that there may be
Someone inside
To give them the food
They so much crave,
They knock.
No one is there—not even a cooking pot.
Bewildered,
Limping slowly along an empty lane,
Their tears fall
Like the rain.

THE FIRST RAIN

Ch'a Shen Hsing (eighteenth century)

Ch'a Shen Hsing was a prodigy who wrote his first verses at
the age of five years.

As soon as the first rain
Has come,
Mortals expect a year of rich harvest.
In general a man comforts himself
With the short view
Before him.
But I look ahead
Even less than the old farmer,
And for me
The first rain merely means
A night of refreshing sleep.

MILITARY TRIUMPH

Kuo Mo Jo (1891–)

How much
Of the people's blood
Has been bartered
For this honor and this glory!
The very thought
—And the tears would flow,
And if one were moved to laughter,
No sound would pass his lips.

VAIN RESOLVES

Wang Man Chün (1901–61)

When man has reached the midway point
On this, the path of life,
He turns his head and slowly looks about.
He has been beset by mountains,
And winding rivers have encircled him.
How many hours of joy have been his lot,
How oft disturbed by fears?
When I ponder on the mistakes that I have made,
I repent, and today I have resolved
To right the wrongs I may have done.
—But how is it possible
For the Great River[1] to flow westward
In its course?

---

[1] The Yangtze River, which flows from west to east.

PETALS IN THE WIND

Liu Hsiao Wei (Liang Dynasty)

The flowers
Are half concealed
By the garden wall.
Even as I watch,
A blossom leaves its parent branch
As though plucked
By the hand of some fair maid.
Ah! How can one prevent
The soft spring wind
From gently blowing?

THE EARLY RISER

Li Tzu Hui (Sung Dynasty)

The village cock has already announced
The coming of the day,
And with the dawn
The moon has gradually grown pale.
Now men pass by, on horseback or on foot.
The post station is empty,
And its lamp has been snuffed out.

POVERTY

Sung Shih

These past years
Dire poverty has been my lot,
And now my house is sold
To my neighbor in the west.
I deeply grieve
As I bid farewell
To the willow
In my eastern garden plot,
For it may look upon me
As a stranger
If perchance we meet again.

THE APE

Wang Man Chih

From my pillow at the west window
I see the cold pond.
At its edge stands an ancient pine.
An ape creeps stealthily
Down to the spring,
Is suddenly startled
At the sight of a shadow
—And runs away.

A NIGHT'S LODGING AT A MOUNTAIN TEMPLE

Chao Feng

Clear moonlight
Among the pines,
A solitary monastery
High amidst the clouds.
Within, a lighted lamp
Before the Buddha's shrine.
A dog barking,
The mountain sunk in autumn sleep.
A late-returning monk
Raps at the gate.

REFLECTIONS

Shao Yang

When last I came,
It was as a traveler
In the green springtime of my life.
Today I return,
An old, white-haired man.
Between the years
A whole generation has passed.
How many successes and failures
It must have seen!

CHANGE

Han Yang

The peach blossoms yearn
To live the whole summer through,
But the winds scatter them,
And the months spare them not.
You may inquire and search
For the men of the generations of Han,
But not one will ever be found.
Dawn after dawn the flowers fall.
Year after year men vanish and change.
Where today
The dust is blown about by the wind,
In ancient times
Surged an ocean deep.

SAD MEMORIES

Tu Hsün Hao

The glory of the moon and the stars
Is obscured by a cloud.
The gloom of the night, the sob of the waves
Bring sadness into my heart.
At midnight, seated before my lamp,
I recall the heartaches
Of the ten years just past,
Brought back now by the rain sweeping in.
How vividly I relive them all!

EARLY TRAVELING

I Ch'ing

From Hundred Flower Field
I can see the capital afar off,
Where the waters of the Hwang Ho flow
Without end.
Under the sky of autumn
The broad empty plain reaches to infinity.
A solitary horseman comes riding toward the west.
I wonder who he may be.

RIDING TO LOYANG

Kung Liang

When we set forth, the stars were still shining,
And even after we had traveled several li,
The sky was not yet bright,
And the clouds and forest could not be distinguished.
The only sounds were those of wind and flowing water.
The moon slipped swiftly down
From the mountaintop.
The river flowed toward the Great Bear
Low in the north.
When we had arrived outside the Great Gate,
Only then did we see, even though dimly,
The great city of Loyang.

WHENCE COMES SPRING?

Po Hsing Ch'ien

You wish to know whence spring does come.
It is born from the virtue of trees
And reveals itself first in secret
To the willows at the gate.
Then it crosses the hills in the darkness,
And the plum awakens.
It melts the silver flowers
That abide in the snow
And releases the rivers from their fetters of ice.
At dawn it arrives
From its sacred home in the east.
At evening it follows the Great Bear
In its path.
It renews and freshens the vast world of the air,
Speeding ever on its way
With a new song in its heart.
It spreads worldwide harmony
Wherever it goes
And needs but the sun's warmth
To mount my terrace steps.

THE STARS AND I

Shen Yüeh

The Milky Way is upright at times,
At others is aslant.
The Great Bear stands or lies upon its side.
As the stars are so inconstant
Who can know what troubles my heart?
By the light of a single lamp
That dimly burns
I weave at my cold loom,
Even though my tears may fall as rain.
To whom can I turn in my grief?
The rooster crows;
The dawn has come.
And I sigh—in vain!

BIBLIOGRAPHY

Abbreviations:
BSOSL: *Bulletin of the School of Oriental Studies*, London.
JNCBRAS: *Journal of the North China Branch, Royal Asiatic Society*, Shanghai.
MSFOS: *Mittheilungen des Seminars für orientalische Sprachen*, Berlin.

Acker, William. *T'ao the Hermit: Sixty Poems by T'ao Ch'ien*. London and New York, 1952.
Acton, Harold, and Ch'en Shih-Hsiang. *Modern Chinese Poetry*. London, 1934.
Alexéev, V. M. *Kitaiskaya poema a poete*. Petrograd, 1916.
Allan, C. Wilfrid. *Makers of Cathay*. 3d ed. Shanghai, 1936.
Allen, Clement F. R. *The Book of Chinese Poetry*. London, 1891.
Ayscough, Florence. "Chinese Poetry and Its Connotations," *JNCBRAS*, Vol. LI, 99.
———. *Chinese Women*. Boston, 1937.
———. *Travels of a Chinese Poet*. London, 1934.
———. *Tu Fu*. London, 1929.
———, and Amy Lowell. *Fir-Flower Tablets*. Boston, 1921.
Ball, J. Dyer. *Rhythms and Rhymes in Chinese Climes*. Hong Kong, 1907.
———. *Things Chinese*. 5th ed. Shanghai, 1925.
Barrow, John. *Travels in China*. 2d ed. London, 1806.
Belpaire, Bruno. *Quarante Poèmes de Li Tai Pó*. Paris, 1921.
Bernhardi, Anna. "Li T'ai Po," *MSFOS*, Vol. XIX, 105.
———. "Tau Jüan-Ming," *MSFOS*, Vol. XVII, 179.
Bernard, Henri. *Sagesse chinoise et philosophie chrètienne*. Tientsin, 1935.
Bethge, Hans. *Die chinesische Flöte*. Leipzig, 1926.
———. *Pfirsichblüten*. Berlin, 1932.
Binyon, Laurence. *The Spirit of Man in Asian Art*. Cambridge, Mass., 1935.

Böhm, Hans. *Lieder aus China*. Munich, 1919.

Brosset, M. *Essai sur le Chi-King*. Paris, 1828.

Brower, Robert H., and Earl Miner. *Japanese Court Poetry*. Stanford, 1961.

Budd, Charles. *Chinese Poems*. Oxford, 1912.

———. "Chinese Poems," *JNCBRAS*, Vol. LXI, 165.

Bynner, Witter, and Kiang Kang-Hu. *The Jade Mountain*. New York, 1929.

———. "A Poem of the Stone Drums (Han Yü)," *China Review* (New York), 1920.

Candlin, Clara M. *The Herald Wind*. London, 1933.

Cheng Chi Yu. *New China in Verse*. Berkeley, 1944.

Chini, M. *Nuvole bianche*. Lanciano, 1918.

Christy, A. B. *Images in Jade*. New York, 1929.

Chung Park Lum. *China Verse*. New York, 1927.

Ch'u Ta Kao. *Chinese Lyrics*. Cambridge, 1937.

Clark, Cyril D. Le Gros. *The Prose Poetry of Su Tung-Po*. Hong Kong, 1935.

———. *Su Tung Po*. London, 1931.

Clementi, Sir Cyril. *Cantonese Love-Songs*. 2 vols. Oxford, 1904.

Colvin, Ian. *After the Chinese*. London, 1927.

Couling, Samuel. *Encyclopedia Sinica*. Shanghai, 1917.

Couvreur, S. *Cheu King*. Ho Kien Fou, 1896.

Cranmer-Byng, L. *The Book of Odes (Shih King)*. London, 1920.

———. *A Feast of Lanterns*. London, 1916.

———. *A Lute of Jade*. London, 1918.

———. *The Never-ending Wrong*. London, 1902.

———. *The Vision of Asia*. London, 1932.

Davis, Sir John. *Poetry of the Chinese*. Macao, 1834; new ed., London, 1870.

De Harlez, C. *La Poésie chinoise*. Brussels, 1892.

D'Hervey Saint-Denys, Marquis. *Le Li-Sao*. Paris, 1870.

———. *Poésies de l'époque des Thang*. Paris, 1862.

Di Giura, L. N. *Poesia de Li Puo*. Lanciano, 1928.

Eitel, E. J. " 'The Shee King,' a Review of Legge's Translation," *Chinese Recorder*.

Erkes, Eduard. *Chinesische Literatur*. Breslau, 1922.

Fang Chêng-Ta. *The Golden Year*. Cambridge, Mass., 1946.

Fitzgerald, C. P. *China: A Short Cultural History*. Rev. ed. London, 1950.

Fletcher, W. J. B. *Gems of Chinese Poetry*. Shanghai, 1917.

———. *More Gems of Chinese Poetry*. Shanghai, 1919.

———. "The Song of a Skirt," *JNCBRAS*, Vol. LII, 193.

———. "A Trip to Kua Kang," *JNCBRAS*, Vol. LII, 192.

Forke, Alfred. *Blüthen chinesischer Dichtung*. 2 vols. Magdeburg, 1899.

———. *Dichtungen der T'ang-und Sung-Zeit*. 2 vols. Hamburg, 1929.

———. "Einige Verse des Wang Wei," *Ostasiatische Zeitschrift*, Vol. II.

Franke, O. *Kêng Tschi Tu*. Hamburg, 1913.

Frodsham, J. D. *The Murmuring Stream*. 2 vols. Kuala Lumpur, 1967.

———., and Ch'eng Hsi, trans. *An Anthology of Chinese Verse: Han Wei Chin and the Northern and Southern Dynasties*. Oxford, 1967.

Gaunt, T. "Ling Yin Monastery Poem," *JNCBRAS*, Vol. LIII, 93.

———. *Little Garden from Cathay*. Shanghai, 1919.

Gauthier, Judith. *Le livre de Jade*. Paris, 1928.

Giles, Herbert A. *A Chinese Biographical Dictionary*. London, 1873.

———. *Chinese Literature*. London, 1901.

———. *Chinese Poetry in English Verse*. London, 1898.

———. *Gems of Chinese Literature: Verse*. Shanghai, 1923.

———. *Two Chinese Poems*. Shanghai, 1873.

———, and Arthur Waley. *Select Chinese Verses*. Shanghai, 1934.

Granet, Marcel. *Festivals and Songs of Ancient China*. London, 1932.

———. *Fêtes et chansons anciennes de la Chine.* Paris, 1929.
———. *La pensée chinoise.* Paris, 1934.
Graves, Stella Maria. *Min River Boat Songs.* New York, 1946.
Grube, Wilhelm. *Geschichte der chinesischen Litteratur.* Leipzig, 1909.
Hammond, Louise Strong. "The Tunes of Chinese Poetry," *Year Book of Oriental Art and Culture* (London), 1924–25.
Hart, Henry H. *A Chinese Market.* Peking and San Francisco, 1931.
———. *A Garden of Peonies.* Stanford, 1938.
———. *The Hundred Names.* Berkeley, 1933.
———. *Poems of the Hundred Names.* 3d ed. Stanford, 1954.
———. *The West Chamber.* Stanford, 1936.
Hauser, Otto. *Die chinesische Dichtung.* Berlin, n.d.
Hawkes, David. *Ch'u Tz'u: The Songs of the South.* Oxford, 1959.
Headland, Isaac Taylor. *Chinese Mother Goose Rhymes.* New York, 1900.
Heilmann, Hans. *Chinesische Lyrik.* Munich, n.d.
Hoffman, Alfred. *Frühlingsblüten und Herbstmond.* Cologne, 1951.
Hsi-Tseng Tsiang. *Poems of the Chinese Revolution.* New York, 1929.
Hsieh Ping Hsin. *Spring Water.* Trans. by Grace M. Boynton. Peking, 1929.
Hubrecht, Alphonse. *Etymologie des caractères chinois.* Peking, 1932.
Hughes, E. R. *Two Chinese Poets.* Princeton, 1960.
———., ed. *The Individual in East and West.* Oxford, 1937.
Hu Hsih. "The Social Message in Chinese Poetry," *Chinese Social and Political Science Review,* Vol. VII.
Hundhausen, Vincenz. *Der Blumengarten von Tang Hsiaen-Dsu.* Peking, 1933.
———. *Chinesische Dichter.* Peking, 1926.

———. *Gedichte von Tau Yüan Ming*. Peking, 1928.

Hung, William. *Tu Fu: China's Greatest Poet*. Cambridge, Mass., 1952.

Ikbal Ali Shah, Sirdar. *The Oriental Caravan*. London, 1933.

Imbault-Huart, Camille. *La poésie chinoise du xivme au xixme siècle*. Paris, 1886.

———. *Poésies modernes chinoises*. Peking, 1892.

———. "Poète chinois du xviiime siècle (Yüan Tseu-ts'ai)," *JNCBRAS*, Vol. XIX, part 2, 1.

Jennings, William. *The Chinese Shi Kingdom*. London, 1891.

Jenyns, Soame. *A Further Selection from the Three Hundred Poems of the T'ang Dynasty*. New York, 1944.

———. *Selections from the Three Hundred Poems of the T'ang Dynasty*. New York, 1940.

Joerissen, Gertrude L. *The Lost Flute*. New York, 1929.

Johns, Francis A. *A Bibliography of Arthur Waley*.

Johnson, Kinchen. *Peiping Rhymes, First Series*. Peking, 1932.

Juan, Marcella de. *Breve Antológia de China*. Madrid, 1948.

Karlgren, Bernhard. *The Poetical Parts in Lao Tsi*. Göteborg, 1932.

———. *Sound and Symbol in Chinese*. Oxford, 1923.

Klabund (pseud. Alfred Henschke). *Dumpfe Trommel und berouschtes Gong*. Leipzig, n.d.

———. *Li-Tai-Pe*. Berlin, n.d.

Kliene, Charles. "The Land of Peach Bloom," *JNCBRAS*, Vol. L, 108.

Koo, T. Z. *Songs of Cathay*. Shanghai, n.d.

———. *Songs of the People*. Shanghai, n.d.

Kratochvil, Paul. *The Chinese Language Today*. London, 1968.

Kurz, Heinrich. *Das Blumenblatt*. St. Gallen, 1836.

La Grasserie, Raoul. *Essai de Métrique chinoise*. Paris, 1893.

Lai Ming. A *History of Chinese Literature*. London, 1964.

Larios, Juan Ruiz de. *Antológia de la Poesia China*. Barcelona, n.d.

Legge, James. *The Book of Poetry*. Shanghai, 1931.

———. *The Chinese Classics*. Vol. IV, parts 1 and 2. Oxford, n.d.

———. *The Sacred Books of China*. Vol. III in *The Sacred Books of the East*. Ed. by Max Müller. Oxford, 1899.

Liang Tsong Tai. *Les Poêmes de T'ao Ts'ien*. Paris, 1930.

Lim Boon Keng. *The Li Sao*. Shanghai, 1929.

Lin Yutang. *The Gay Genius (Su Tung Po)*. New York, 1947.

Liu Wu-Chi. *An Introduction to Chinese Literature*. Bloomington, 1966.

Luh, C. W. *On Chinese Poetry*. Peking, 1935.

Mackintosh, Duncan, and Alan Ayling. *A Collection of Chinese Lyrics*. London, 1965.

Manent, Maria. *L'aire Daurat*. Barcelona, 1946.

Martin, W. A. P. *The Lore of Cathay*. New York, 1912.

Mayers, William F. *The Chinese Readers' Manual*. Shanghai, 1924.

Medhurst, W. H. "Chinese Poetry," *China Review*, Vol. IV.

Mote, F. W. *The Poet Kao Ch'i*. Princeton, 1962.

Musso, Giuseppe D. *La Cina ed I Cinese*. 2 vols. Milan, 1926.

Obata, Shigeyoshi. *Li Po*. New York, 1922.

———. *The Works of Li Po*. Orient ed. Tokyo, 1935.

Oehler-Heimerdinger, Elisabeth. *Das Frauenherz*. Stuttgart, n.d.

Okada, Tetsuzo. *Chinese and Sino-Japanese Poems*. Tokyo, 1937.

Pai Ta-Shuh. *Chinese Lyrics*. New York, 1916.

Parke, E. H. *John Chinaman*. London, 1902.

Pauthier, G. "De la Poésie chinoise," *La Revue encyclopédique* (Paris), February, 1933.

Payne, Robert, ed. *Contemporary Chinese Poetry*. London, 1947.
——. *The White Pony*. New York, 1947.
Pfizmaier, August. *Elegische Dichtung der Chinesien*. Vienna, 1887.
Plath, Jo. *Ueber zwei Sammlungen chinesischer Gedichte aus des Dynastie Thang*. Munich, 1869.
Pound, Ezra. *Cathay*. London, 1915.
Purcell, V. W. W. *The Spirit of Chinese Poetry*. Singapore, 1929.
Rückert, Friedrich. *Schi-King: Chinesisches Liederbuch*. Altona, 1833.
Seubert, Adolf. *Chinesische Gedichte*. Leipzig, n.d.
Shih Shun Liu. *One Hundred and One Chinese Poems*. Hong Kong and Oxford, 1967.
Sié Kong. *L'Amour maternel dans la Littérature féminine en Chine*. Paris, 1937.
Soong, Tsung Faung. *La Littérature chinoise contemporaine*. Peking, 1919.
Soulié de Morant, George. *Anthologie de l'amour chinois*. Paris, 1932.
——. *Essai sur la littérature chinoise*. Paris, 1921.
——. *Florilège des poèmes Song*. Paris, 1923.
Stent, George Carter. "Chinese Lyrics," *JNCBRAS*, Vol. VI, 93.
——. *Entombed Alive*. London, 1878.
——. *The Jade Chaplet*. London, 1874.
Sung-Nien Hsu. *Anthologie de la littérature chinoise*. Paris, 1933.
——. "Quelques poèmes de Tou Fou," *Revue Franco-Chinoise*, Vol. XII, Nos. 3 and 4 (Paris), 1931.
Tchang, Fong. *Le Paon*. Paris, 1924.
Tchou, Kia-Kien, and Armond Gandon. *Anthologie de la poésie chinoise*. Peking, 1927.
Tietjens, Eunice, ed. *Poetry of the Orient*. New York, 1928.
Toussaint, Franz. *La flûte de jade*. Paris, n.d.

Trevelyan, R. C., ed. *From the Chinese*. Oxford, 1945.

Tsên Tsonming. *Anciens poèmes chinois d'auteurs inconnus*. Lyons, 1929.

——. *Essai historique sur la poésie chinoise*. Lyons, 1922.

——. *Une goutte d'eau*. Paris, 1925.

——. *Histoire de la poésie chinoise*. Shanghai, 1936.

——. *Rêve d'une nuit d'hiver*. Lyons, 1922.

Underwood, Edna Worthley, and Chi Hwang Chu. *Tu Fu: Wanderer and Minstrel Under Moons of Cathay*. Portland, Maine, 1929.

Van Doren, Mark. *An Anthology of World Poetry*. New York, 1928.

Vissière, A. "Les herbes (Po Chü I)," *Bulletin de l'association amicale franco-chinoise*, Vol. I.

——. "Le Poète Tou Fou," *Bulletin de l'association amicale franco-chinoise*, Vol. I.

——. "Quelques mots sur la poésie chinoise," *Revue franco-chinoise*, Vol. X, No. 3.

Vitale, Guido. *Pekinese Rhymes*. Peking, 1896.

Waddell, Helen. *Lyrics from the Chinese*. London, 1914.

Waley, Arthur. *The Book of Songs*. 2 vols. London, 1937.

——. *Chinese Poems*. London, 1946.

——. "Further Poems of Po Chu-I," *BSOSL*, 1918.

——. "Hymns to Kuan-Yin," *BSOSL*, 1920.

——. *The Life and Times of Po Chü-I*. London, 1949.

——. *More Translations from the Chinese*. New York, 1919.

——. *The Nine Songs*. London, 1955.

——. "Notes on Chinese Prosody, *Journal of the Royal Asiatic Society*, April, 1918.

——. *170 Chinese Poems*. New York, 1919.

——. *Poems from the Chinese*. London, n.d.

——. *Poet Li Po*. London, 1918.

——. *The Poetry and Career of Li Po*. London, 1950.

——. "Pre-T'ang Poetry," *BSOSL*, 1917.

——. *The Temple*. New York, n.d.

———. "Thirty-eight Poems by Po Chü-I," *BSOSL*, 1917.
  Note: The various editions of Arthur Waley's books contain enlightening prefaces and introductions.
Wang Ching-Wei. *Poems*. London, 1938.
Wang Tsang Pao. *La femme dans la société chinoise*. Paris, 1933.
Watson, Burton. *Early Chinese Literature*. New York, 1962.
Watters, T. *Essays on the Chinese Language*. Shanghai, 1889.
———. "Life and Works of Han Yü, or Han Wên Kung," *JBCBRAS*, Vol. VII, 165.
Werner, E. T. C. *Chinese Ditties*. Tientsin, 1922.
———. *Chinese Sociology*. London, 1910.
———. *A Dictionary of Chinese Mythology*. Shanghai, 1932.
———. *Myths and Legends of China*. New York, 1922.
Whitall, James. *Chinese Lyrics*. New York, 1923.
Whymant, A. Neville J. "Chinese Coolie Songs," *BSOSL*, 1920.
Wieger, Léon. *Caractères chinois*. 4th ed. Hsien Hsien, 1924.
———. *Chinese Characters*. Hsien Hsien, 1927.
Wilder, J. D., and J. H. Ingram. *Analysis of Chinese Characters*. Peking, 1921.
Wilhelm, Richard. *Chinesisch-deutsche Jahres-und Tageszeiten*. Jena, 1922.
———. *Die chinesische Literatur*. Potsdam, 1926.
Williams, E. T. *China Yesterday and Today*. 5th ed. New York, 1932.
Williams, S. Wells. *The Middle Kingdom*. Rev. ed. New York, 1913.
Williamson, H. R. *Wang An Shih*. Peking, 1935.
———. *Wang An Shih*. 2 vols. London, 1937.
Wimsatt, Genevieve. *Selling Wilted Peonies*. New York, 1936.

Woitsch, L. *Aus den Gedichten Po Chü-i*. Leipzig, 1916.

———. *Lieder eines chinesischen Dichters und Trinkers (Po Chü-i)*. Leipzig, 1925.

Wylie, Alexander. *Notes on Chinese Literature*. Shanghai, 1922.

Yoshikawa, Kojiro. *An Introduction to Sung Poetry*. Trans. by Burton Watson. Cambridge, Mass., 1967.

Zottoli, Angelo. *Cursus litteraturae Sinicae neo-missionariis accomodatu*. Vol. V. Shanghai, 1882.

INDEX OF POETS

The paper on which this book is printed bears the watermark of the University of Oklahoma Press and has an effective life of at least three hundred years.